Say Hi To Jesus For Me

Gabriele Monson

AUGSBURG Publishing House • Minneapolis

Foreword

"A time to weep, and a time to laugh; a time to mourn, and a time to dance; . . . a time to get, and a time to lose" (Ecc. 3:4, 6 KJV).

Reading this book tore me apart.

It was a shattering experience, like none other in my life. I became involved with the Monsons and their beautiful son. I hoped against hope, I prayed (though I knew the events I was reading about had already become history), and finally I was sobbing uncontrollably. I put the book down, because I couldn't bear it any longer.

I came back to it, because I had to know the rest of the story. Within a moment I found myself sobbing out loud again. It was painful, it was heartrending, it was shattering.

Then why would I want you to read it? Why would I want *everybody*, especially moms and dads, to read this story?

Because it's beautiful. Because it's true. Because it could happen to any of us. And mainly, because in this story you'll meet Jesus.

It's his story, as well as Todd's. He's been through this valley, and he went through it again with the Monsons.

Now when I read the 23rd Psalm, I have a much better sense of who the Good Shepherd is. I better understand the valley of the shadow of death and the rod and the staff that lead and comfort.

As you'll see, that's why Gabriele wanted to tell this story. She's not just weeping for her child, though she has the right to do that. She wants people to know the Shepherd who led her through this dark vale. It was this Shepherd who said in Luke 6:21: "Blessed (happy!) are ye that weep now; for ye shall laugh" (KJV).

Jesus wept—and he wants us to.

In Romans 12:15 he commands: "Rejoice with them that do rejoice, and weep with them that weep" (KJV). Why? Well, I'm finding that, in all of God's commandments, the directive is for our own good.

We need to weep. I have been changed by

Todd's story. I feel closer to the Lord, and much more compassionate toward my brothers and sisters, and all those who suffer in any way.

And more than ever, I despise the one "who comes but to rob, to kill and to destroy"—the accuser of the brethren, the father of all liars, the adversary of God. Satan is the author of death, the enemy of our souls, the source of evil. Reading this story has made me want, more than ever before in my life, to have nothing at all to do with him.

Surely this must be one of the reasons God allows suffering, even in innocent children. Didn't he challenge Abraham to sacrifice his own firstborn son? Wasn't that just a preview of a time when man's sin would rob God himself of *his* firstborn? And if it weren't for reminders all around us of the consequences and the dread price of sin, wouldn't we all become complacent toward it? What can impress upon us more starkly the eternal horror of sin than the agony and death of an innocent child? Sadly, we *need* that price tag held up before our eyes from time to time—and it's written in real flesh and blood.

But there's a happy and triumphant aspect to this story, too.

Jim Elliot, the missionary who was murdered by the same Auca Indians he went to serve, once said, "God is peopling heaven; should we deny him the laughter and joy of children there?"

Jesus came into the house where the little girl had died and asked, "Why make ye this ado, and weep? The damsel is not dead, but sleepeth" (Mark 5:39 KJV). He knew the child would arise, and he knew that he himself was to triumph over death, hell, and the grave, and that he would bring that child—and all who trust in him—into his own eternal home. He promises in Revelation 21:4 that there will be no weeping there.

I'm looking forward to laughing with Jesus and Todd and his folks.

PAT BOONE

Preface

Why did I write this book?

Corrie ten Boom expressed our experience and our feelings when she said, "There is no pit so deep that he is not deeper still."

It is tempting for us to look back and wonder what we could have done differently. It is not the point of this book to say that we handled everything perfectly, but to share our humanness and to show how God took us by the hand and led us through our valley.

This book is written:

• as a tribute to our Lord and God, who was able to bring us through the hell of losing our child and who, as we keep looking to him, will bring us through anything life may bring our way—one step at a time.

• as a tribute to all our brothers and sisters in Christ, who gave of themselves through their love and prayers.

• as a tribute to all those who will come to trust Jesus as they walk through their valley with him.

• as a tribute to Todd, whose childlike love for Jesus so greatly enriched our lives.

• and, lest we forget.

GABRIELE MONSON

1

We were busy trying to get Todd into Little League, even though he was not old enough to join. Dutch had always said that when Todd was older he would play more ball with him and even coach a team. Then, mostly while we were not watching, Todd kept busy practicing until one day we discovered he could pitch quite well. Under our eyes had blossomed an all-American, blond, blue-eyed, baseball-loving boy.

Todd had endless energy, swam like a fish, and was proud of being the fastest runner. When he got a pair of tennis shoes, he made sure they were the "fast-running" kind. He was also proud to be a good student. He was a crazy kid who, when he had a loose baby tooth, talked a friend into punching him in the mouth to knock it out. He ate and ate, as much as his father almost, and never seemed to gain any weight, quite contrary to the rest of us.

Then one day the school nurse called and said Todd had vomited and could I pick him up? I didn't have a car, but school was only a few blocks from our house, so I walked down to get him.

He assured me that he felt better and that he was well enough to walk home. We stopped in his classroom so I could ask his teacher what had happened. She told me that he had seemed to have violent stomach cramps and that he'd vomited just as they stepped out the door on the way to the nurse's office.

We walked home together in a slow, leisurely manner, joking and laughing along the way. Close to home I noticed that his pants were wet again. He had been having a problem with wetting, and nothing we did or said seemed to make any difference.

I decided to put him to bed, hoping rest would cure his flu. But then I discovered his pants were soaked with blood. Alarmed, I called the doctor. The nurse suggested bringing him in right away. But Dutch had the car, and I wasn't sure where he was. By co-(God)-incidence, I located him at a store he'd stopped by, and he rushed home to transport us to the doctor.

I sat in the waiting room with our daughter, Niqua, while Dutch accompanied Todd into the examining room. Dutch had not seen the blood, so neither he nor the doctor was aware of the amount of blood Todd had lost. The doctor suspected that Todd had an infection and that he may have coughed and ruptured a blood vessel.

When I heard this, I went back in to tell the doctor just how much blood Todd had lost. She asked that we collect some urine samples and bring Todd back the next day.

The samples we took seemed to be nothing but blood. When the doctor saw them the next day, she ordered Todd into the hospital immediately.

Todd cried. He was frightened, and so was I. I didn't quite know how to reassure him. For a few moments, we just held each other, trying to find comfort. Then we remembered: No matter where we are or what happens, Jesus is always with us.

The diagnosis was nephritis. But the doctor said, "There's a small chance that it's a tumor." That went in one ear and out the other. Who ever heard of a tumor in a child! Besides, things like that always happen to other people, never to us.

Lately, the Lord's Prayer kept returning to my attention. First, during a memorial service, it sent shivers down my spine. After that, it seemed every time I got into my car and turned on the radio, there it was. I had begun to suspect that God was trying to tell me something. I even mentioned my suspicion to my Bible study group. But I was a brand-new Christian, just rescued from tranquilizers by the saving blood of Jesus, and I did not yet know much about God's guidance.

Now I had my answer. God *had* been trying to tell me something, and this was it. Todd had nephritis. He was in the hospital for the first time. I marveled at how God had prepared me so we would know he was with us.

Todd settled into the hospital routine fast. He made friends with the nurses even faster. He was soon helping them at the desk. I stayed with him during the day. He spent the time playing, and beating me at spelling games. Dutch stayed with him the first night.

The second day Todd seemed much better. We played ball in the hall and he had a great time. The doctor even gave us hope that he might come home by the weekend.

The second night we decided to leave him alone. When we left, he was busy playing. But we'd just arrived home when he called. "Please, Mom, come. I can't sleep alone."

It seemed so cruel to leave him there pleading, but I was sure he would be sound asleep by the time I could drive back to the hospital. We talked on the phone for half an hour. I prayed with him, then asked him to settle down in bed and turn the TV off, hoping to talk to him until he went to sleep. I waited on the other end while a nurse helped him to the bathroom and then back to bed. He finally said he was tired enough to sleep.

He seemed fine the next day, but he spent more time in bed. He lay there looking out the window. It was a brilliantly clear day and the wind was playing with big white balls of clouds. Todd was deep in thought.

Finally he said: "Mom, are the dead people up there in those clouds? Can they see us?"

He'd been thinking a lot about heaven. Just a short time before, we'd had to have his first very own puppy dog put to sleep. When I told Todd that King had gone to heaven, he cried. But soon his little mind tried to form a picture of what it was like for King.

"Mom, do they have balls in heaven? Do you think God will play ball with him now?"

"Mom, if the ball falls down from heaven, is God going to come down and pick it up for him?"

We reflected on God and talked awhile. He was in pain and finally had to have a shot. I

13

noticed that he seemed to be bleeding more, and I asked the nurse to bring a pad for the bed. She was alarmed at the blood and called the doctor.

The doctor ordered X rays immediately. While they were being taken, she said she was glad Dutch had gone home so she could talk to me alone. She knew how upset Dutch became at the slightest hint of one of us being ill.

She said she had to tell me that we now must seriously consider the possibility of a tumor. She meant it when she said she was sorry. She advised transferring Todd to the Children's Hospital, where he would be treated by a urologist. I agreed.

I called Dutch's cousin Betty and asked her to try to find Dutch. I also called Pastor Roufs. He came right away to pray with me and support me, and he allowed me to cry. Betty came too, and brought some lunch.

By the time Dutch arrived, Todd was feeling quite poorly and was bleeding more and more. The doctor thought an ambulance might be traumatic for Todd, so we bundled him up carefully and headed for the Children's Hospital in our car, a very frightened threesome. Betty and her husband Harvey saw us off. They even had a present for Todd.

A doctor was waiting for us. He examined Todd at length. Todd was bleeding constantly now, and he was in pain. It seemed to take forever to get him admitted.

In the waiting room I leafed through an old copy of *Reader's Digest*. There it was again! An article on the Lord's Prayer. I held it up for Dutch to see. "Look! Now what?" Inwardly I recoiled from the blow I knew would come.

2

We took turns that night sleeping on the couch in Todd's room and sitting up with him.

I had a tape recorder in the drawer of Todd's nightstand. Softly I played a tape of a recent service. It was barely audible, but it gave the room an air of worship.

For a long time I sat in the waiting room and listened to the night noises of the hospital. During the day the sixth floor had been quite a busy place—doctors, nurses, technicians, and parents hurrying around, and children who were well enough to be out of bed roaming the halls on their scooters, wagons, and wheelchairs. We heard their laughter as well as their cries.

But at night the sounds were different. The

boy in the room next to ours was on a heart monitor. His heartbeat was very irregular. Beep .....beep ....beepbeep ....beep ..... beepbeepbeepbeep .... beep........... When there was a pause, I prayed that another beep would follow. Then the monitor raced and the beeps were almost one continual sound.

Here and there I heard children crying. Some were lonely; others were in pain.

My heart cried out to God: "Don't you hear these children crying? Where are you while all this is going on? Please help."

The answer came in the quietness of my heart, the assurance that he was there and that he knew. I felt his sadness, and especially his loving presence.

The next day brought tests upon tests. And always the doctor's explanations: "These tests carry a certain amount of risk. This and that could happen. But we need them." We signed each consent form.

The first test results were in. There was a tumor on Todd's left kidney.

"A tumor!" The information sank in only bit by bit. The doctors knew of our need to receive information and comprehend slowly. They only answered the questions we were ready to ask.

"Well then, is it malignant?" We hardly dared ask.

"Yes? . . . Well then, will you have to take the kidney?" They said they would, but assured us that Todd could get along perfectly well with one kidney.

Now more tests had to be taken. They advised us to go home, since Todd would be sedated and we could not be with him anyway.

We left in a state of shock. In the car we cried as we realized "malignant" meant that dreaded disease: *cancer.* Our world came crashing in.

I thought I remembered that God had promised not to allow us to be tempted more than we are able to endure. When we got home, I pulled out our Bible and found the verse: "No temptation has overtaken you that is not common to man. God is faithful, and he will not let you be tempted beyond your strength, but with the temptation will also provide the way of escape, that you may be able to endure it" (1 Cor. 10:13).

I told Dutch, "I don't know about you, but this is what I'm going to hang on to."

We made some phone calls. My mother was visiting relatives in Germany. We had called her earlier in the week to say Todd was in the hospital. Now we called again.

My cousin answered. "Yes," he said, "your mother is with us, but she's out trying to make arrangements for a flight home. It's very difficult to get the proper connections."

"Michael, please tell her to come home right away. Toddy has cancer."

Silence.

"Michael, did you hear me? Toddy has cancer. Will you tell mother?"

"Yes, yes, I'll tell her."

Mother said later that when she got back Michael turned pale and could hardly bring out the words to tell her.

We tried to sleep, but soon went back to the hospital. Pastor Roufs was there with us again to hear the test results.

The doctor drew us a picture of the tumor surrounding the kidney and explained how they planned to remove it the next morning. Tears came to my eyes. I guess I had been putting up a good front, because Pastor Roufs was caught off guard when I broke down and cried.

We didn't tell Todd much when he arrived back in his room. We tried to assure him that everything would be OK.

Around midnight the nurse put a tag on Todd's bed and explained that he was to have nothing by mouth before surgery. No water—nothing.

When morning came Dutch talked to the doctor one more time and asked him to please do all that he could. The doctor put his arms around Dutch and said, "We have children too." That was all we needed to hear to know he would do his best.

When the nurse came to take Todd to surgery, we went along as far as the elevator. He cried and didn't want to go. In the elevator he told the nurse he thought he was going to die.

The hours of waiting dragged on. Friends came to help us pass the time. Harvey even took off work to be with Dutch.

Our inner turmoil was great. I burst out at my friend Pam, "I do want the will of God for our lives, but not if it means that Todd has to die!"

Finally we received word that all had gone well and that Todd would soon be out of recovery and back in his room.

The doctor reported that the tumor had been very large, about three times the size of the kidney, but that it had been fully encapsulated. Also, lymph glands right next to the kidney were completely free of disease. That offered much hope for Todd's complete recovery, since there was no visible evidence of the cancer having spread any further.

I looked forward to Todd's return from surgery with a certain amount of fear. I didn't know what to expect, what he would look like, and I dreaded seeing the wound.

He was pale and sleepy when he came, this little boy who was always so full of energy. He took shallow breaths. An IV was hooked to his arm. We had to move him very carefully.

He was in pain. Every move hurt. We forced on him the first injection for pain. When it was time for the next one, he fought hard, throwing himself around the bed to escape it. He became hysterical, pleading: "Please, Mom!"

"The shot just hurts for a little while, but then you will be more comfortable," I said.

"No, *please*. I'll just hold your hand and squeeze it real hard when it hurts."

The doctor thought that if Todd felt so strongly about it he should be allowed to try to get along without injections. So Todd lay there and shivered from the pain. His knuckles turned white from squeezing my hand, but he kept right on refusing the shots.

Later, we found out why. When his dog King had been ill, we were careful not to mention the terms "put to sleep" and "shots" to him. We simply told him King had gone to heaven. *(Dear Lord, are there animals in heaven?)* But he must have heard us talk to others about King, for now he thought we were trying to give him shots to have him put to sleep also. That's why he was willing to endure the pain.

3

That night my mother came to the hospital straight from the airport. Her presence gave me new strength. We went home together to get a few hours of sleep while Dutch stayed with Todd. But sleep wouldn't come. We had so much to catch up on and to cry over.

Finally, late that night, I was able to pray, "Yes, Lord. Thy will be done, no matter what." I realize now that I automatically associated God's will with a negative answer to my prayers.

At the hospital in the morning we found that Todd had been assigned a physical therapist who was to turn him frequently and get him to sit up in bed. Todd was so pale as he lay sleeping. Since I had given him to the Lord, all I wanted was for him to die peacefully, drifting off in his sleep. And now this nurse wanted to get him up! We argued with her and tried to get her to leave him alone. "Can't you see that he's sick? Come back some other day."

The head nurse came and explained to us that the longer Todd waited to get up, the harder it would be for him. Besides, the risk of his getting pneumonia was greater if he wasn't active.

Mother and I realized we weren't helping Todd by hovering over him. We went to the cafeteria to unwind and talked for quite a while, leaving the tension of the hospital room behind.

When we got back, the therapist had succeeded in getting Todd to sit at the edge of his bed, dangling his feet for a short while. Todd was tired, but proud. She continued to work with Todd all day, getting him up at regular intervals, taking him a little further each time.

When it was time for him to get out of bed completely, he asked us all to leave. He was going to do it alone.

Anxiously we stood in front of the door to his room, knowing he couldn't. But then the door opened, and out came Todd. We cheered and applauded.

One arm was immobilized by a board to keep the IV needle in the vein, so he had trouble deciding how he could both push his IV pole and hold up his pants (which were forever falling down). But he was walking!

"Thank you, Lord!" I felt as if Todd had been given back to us. When I gave him to the Lord, I had been sure he was going to die, and here he was, walking down the hall, all the way to the phone booth to call Grandma and Grandpa in Iowa. Praise the Lord!

During the long nights and days at the hospital, I started work on a blanket to help pass the time. I learned to carry my yarn and crochet hook with me at all times. Often I would even crochet in the dark, so Todd and his roommate wouldn't be disturbed by the light. I call that blanket the product of my sleepless nights.

The Bible tells us to keep our minds on things above. I kept a tape of church music playing softly in Todd's room. Even though we weren't always conscious of the music, our minds absorbed it, helping us focus our thoughts on Jesus. When the atmosphere in other rooms was tense, ours was usually calm and filled with the presence of God.

Later I prayed about having a radio to replace the tape recorder. A friend soon supplied one, and it went with us from then on.

I was a babe in Christ, but we came to find out that Todd was not. He had gone to church school for two and a half years, and he'd had a devout and devoted teacher who transmitted her love for the Lord to the children. This along with Sunday school gave Todd a faith from which he was now drawing.

Often as Todd had left for school, I had told him, "Take Jesus with you. Jesus is with you wherever you go. He will never leave you." He knew this when he went for surgery. He knew it all through his illness.

Always at night before Todd went to sleep, I would say to him, "Goodnight, son. See you in the morning. Say hi to Jesus for me in your dreams."

Todd's principal and his teacher came to see him at different times during his recovery. They brought cards, pictures, and greetings from the children at school. I punched a hole in each card and picture, threaded a length of yarn through them, and hung them on the walls. Soon the room looked bright and cheerful.

Todd was so proud that the principal would take time to play a spelling game with him. They had quite a contest. The principal even promised to take him to McDonald's for lunch as soon as Todd was back in school. McDonald's! With the principal!

Todd loved to play a game that had a bubble in the middle with dice inside. Players have to press the bubble down to get the dice to jump. First we had to press the bubble for Todd;

then we helped him press it. How proud he was when he had the strength to press it all by himself.

Soon it was time to make more decisions. We were asked to join the nurse coordinator and the hematologist, whom I'll call Dr. Nelson, in the conference room.

All visible cancer had been removed surgically. Now the invisible cells had to be attacked. We were asked to decide if we wanted chemotherapy only, or with cobalt treatments. The doctors knew of no advantage either way. Since there was no obvious advantage to be gained from cobalt in Todd's case, we decided against it, but we had no choice but to go along with chemotherapy. I was startled when they said they should start treatments the very next day.

The therapy was to be given by intravenous injection. But they couldn't do that! Todd was so afraid of shots that he had refused them, even in pain. How could we possibly get him to hold still for these?

We asked the doctor to send someone, a psychiatrist, if necessary, to talk with Todd and explain to him exactly why the injections had to be given. Perhaps if he knew more about what was going on it would be easier for him to take.

We all walked back to Todd's room, and Dr.

Nelson sat on Todd's bed. He took great care to explain to Todd as best he could the injection he would have to have. He won Todd's trust and they were good friends from then on. Todd still did not like the thought of the injections, but he no longer believed they would kill him.

The faces in the sixth-floor waiting room changed every day, but the scene was largely the same. Besides serving sixth-floor patients, it was also the place where parents waited for word on their children in surgery and in intensive care. Every night people lay sleeping on couches and even on the floor. I brought some air mattresses from home, and they were put to good use.

Once as I was talking to a couple I discovered that we not only had a sick child in common, but also our love for God. I got my tape recorder and played a Kathryn Kuhlman tape for them. The waiting room was full and people were watching TV, so I kept the volume very low. I was self-conscious and timid about playing religious music in a public place. But people started singing along with the music and turned the volume up. For a moment the waiting room became a sanctuary. Then my new friends were called away and didn't return.

It was sad to see children face surgery all alone. In many cases, parents lived too far away or could not take time off from work to be with their children. Some little guys and gals tried to be brave; others screamed in fear.

A boy in the neighboring room rarely had visitors. He was lonesome and often cried. He was thin and seemed quite ill. Mother or I would go over and sit with him and hold his hand, which lay limp. What a joy it was when he at last responded with a slight squeeze of his hand. It was as if strength was flowing from our bodies to his.

We heard rumors about the fourth floor where the children went to die. I'm sure everyone pictured it as a dark, gloomy hall, with death looming everywhere.

The sixth floor was the "surgical" floor, so many children were there for simple corrective surgery. It seemed strange to hear mothers worry about "little" things like tonsils or appendixes. What did they know about problems? Our son had *cancer*.

The Lord showed me later that he is just as concerned about a runny nose or a broken arm as he is about major illness. He reminded me of how worried I was when our daughter Niqua was hospitalized with a bladder infection.

The day Todd was discharged, we ran about excitedly, getting our things together, signing discharge papers, and saying all our good-byes. We were going home!

4

The doctors said Todd would have to have chemotherapy for at least two years after all absence of disease. I was sure no more cancer would ever be found. It had been a close call, but we had placed Todd in God's hands, and God had given him back to us. Praise the Lord! Now I wanted to get on with the business of living. I was quite annoyed with the doctors for insisting on the chemotherapy. But there was nothing I would or could do about it. At least the injections were scheduled for only one week out of every two months.

The first clinic visit after Todd's discharge was for chemotherapy only. Todd screamed and kicked, trying to fight off the nurses who had to give the shot. I felt like explaining, "You

31

don't understand. He has cancer. He has been through a lot. Please be patient with him." I thought we were the only ones with that problem.

But the nurse had worked there many years, and she had been through this countless times. She knew this was just the first of many times for us. When we left, she asked that Todd wear slippers or soft shoes the next time. He had hurt her, kicking her with his street shoes.

I was eager to get Todd to a Kathryn Kuhlman miracle service. At each service I had attended, I'd felt the Lord so near, and I'd cried for joy with those who received healing. I longed to stand again in the crowds with my arms uplifted, singing: "Hallelujah!"

Dutch agreed that we could take Todd to a miracle service, but it was against his wishes. At that time he had not yet met his Lord, even though he had always seemed to be the "religious" one in the family. I felt that I was blamed that we hadn't gone to church for some years.

To get into the auditorium for an afternoon service, people started forming a line as early as 6:00 A.M. We usually tried to get there no later than 8:30 or 9:00 A.M.

Todd was still in pain from the surgery. To get to his kidney, the doctors had had to temporarily push aside intestines, and that was still causing him pain. We did not think he could stand to wait in line so many hours.

We called the woman who chartered the bus to take people from our area to the service. Demand was so great that usually all seats were spoken for weeks ahead of time. But we explained our situation to her, and she somehow was able to get us two seats on the next bus. Todd would have to sit on our laps.

After the bus ride and the long wait in line, Todd was tired and in pain again. Dutch had to carry Todd to keep up with the rushing crowd. Someone told the usher. He said he would watch over Todd for any sign of the power of God upon him.

I came full of hope. I had witnessed so many wonderful healings. In reading the Gospels, I knew that Jesus healed then, and since he is the same yesterday, today, and forever, I knew that he healed today.

"Here is my boy, Lord. He is yours, too. His body is broken. Make him whole, please. Make his scar from surgery disappear so the doctors will know that a miracle has happened. I don't *ever* want him to have to have any more of that chemotherapy. Thy will be done, Lord, on earth as it is in heaven."

We finally gave Todd some Tylenol for the pain. After a while he went to sleep and started to perspire heavily. We were all so preoccupied with Todd, we gave no thought to the service, or to God for that matter. Dutch was annoyed and I was anxious.

I knew nothing was impossible for God. He had made us, so he certainly could fix us when we were broken. But would he do it for Todd?

Besides hoping for healing, I was also eager for Dutch to like the service. I wanted him to feel the joy and the closeness to the Lord that I felt.

Todd woke up and was entirely pain-free for the first time that day. The ushers encouraged us to step out in the hall to see if anything had happened. But Todd was so tired of our fussing over him, he stepped into a phone booth, closed the door, and refused to come out until we left him alone.

Dutch decided it was time to go home. I was so disappointed! Everything had gone wrong!

Oh, I knew that Todd was healed. Of course he was. But I needed proof.

The doctors had said that because Todd's tumor was encapsulated and the adjacent lymph nodes were "clean," there was a 90% chance Todd would be all right. I wanted God to finish the job, to make it 100%, to throw in a new kidney and remove the scar. I just could not face two years of chemotherapy. I wanted proof of healing for the doctors. I thought then that they were in conflict with God's purpose.

Later I saw that the doctors were instruments of God.

Todd continued to recover. Soon he was back in school, having a good time. I was still frustrated by the lack of proof of his healing. Yet I was confident that all would be well.

The next time we took Todd to a miracle service, he was feeling fine. Again I prayed for healing, but this time I was absorbed in singing praises to God from the depth of my heart. Thousands of us stood singing "Hallelujah!"

Todd was standing in the aisle with another child. I turned, and there he was, with uplifted arms, uplifted face, singing "Hallelujah!" What greater gift could I ask for?

Miss Kuhlman often said that more important than physical healing was spiritual healing. My usual response to that was "Nuts! What can be more important than to be able to walk again after spending years in a wheelchair, than receiving sight after having been blind, than hearing after having been deaf, than speaking after having been mute?"

But here was Todd, oblivious to his surroundings, praising God. Suddenly I knew what Kathryn had been talking about.

I was growing in the Lord every day, learning to love him more and more. But the more I grew, the more concerned I was that Dutch did not know the Lord the way I knew him.

We had joined a church a few months earlier because we felt it was "the thing to do" to bring the children up right. I assumed that everything was all right now that we belonged, but I kept wondering why the pastor singled me out during all the sermons. Why was he directing his words at me?

I had always tried to be good, striving to live by the Golden Rule. At night sleep wouldn't come unless I prayed the German equivalent of "Now I lay me down to sleep." I had been baptized and confirmed and raised in a Christian family. No one was more right with God than I was.

But finally the words Jesus spoke, recorded in the Bible, created in my heart a longing to know him better.

One day at a Bible study I interrupted the discussion: "That's right! Salvation is a free gift of God. There is nothing you can do to earn it. You must simply accept it from Jesus."

The coin had dropped. I understood.

That afternoon I dreamed that Jesus had taken me high in the air in what seemed to be a translucent bubble. He showed me the whole world and said: "It's all yours. It's my gift to you."

After that I had such peace and inner joy. Many times Dutch caught me smiling and deep in thought. "What are you smiling about?"

Until that time I had been on a daily dose of Valium. Some days I had felt so "calm" that I couldn't drive a car. Other days I just spent crying. So Dutch didn't know what to think of his new, smiling wife. "What are you smiling about?"

"Oh, I just can't help it. All I can think about is Jesus," I answered. The longing in my heart was fulfilled.

I couldn't help but feel, though, that Dutch did not know the Lord the way that I did now. One day I told him so. "You are not a Christian. Just because you went to church most of your life, and even taught Sunday school, does not mean you're a Christian. The Bible says you have to be born again, and I don't think you have been. Tell me, if you died today, do you know for sure that you'd go to heaven? And what are you going to cite as reasons for him letting you in?"

If I wanted to fight, this was a good way to start. "I'm not *that* bad, you know," he growled. But it did give him food for thought. I began to pray for him, for his salvation. I had visions of how I would fall on my knees in front of everyone when the day came on which Dutch asked Jesus to be Lord of his life. I left his car radio tuned to a religious radio station, hoping he would listen; left Christian books lying around, hoping he would read them; dropped every hint I could, and asked others to pray for him also.

He only sank into deeper depression. Todd's medical bills were piling up. We had good insurance, but the small expenses were accumulating, along with the costs of eating out and all the extra things that went with hospitalization. Dutch was back and forth to the hospital all the time, so his work suffered. And, of course, his thoughts were with Todd.

He had many nightmares. One night he woke me and asked me to stay up with him. He said he was tempted to commit suicide. He felt as if God and Satan were fighting over him and he was being torn apart between them. I asked him to accept Jesus into his life. He said he couldn't, that he didn't know how and didn't understand what it would mean.

In the end, all my efforts to win Dutch to the Lord made less of an impression on him than two simple changes in my life. First, I was off tranquilizers. Second, I made the commitment to him that as head of our house he would have the last word from now on. He could hardly get over that. "It took a lot of guts for you to say that."

Jesus said, "If the Son makes you free, you will be free indeed." "Old things are passed away; behold, all things are become new" (KJV). Dutch saw that I was a new creature in Christ, and he longed to know Jesus as I knew him.

One day when I was at the hospital with Todd, Dutch called. His voice sounded different—all choked up, but in a joyful way. He said he had a wonderful surprise for me, but he couldn't tell me until he got to the hospital.

When he arrived, he said he hadn't been able to sleep again the night before. He'd picked up Pat Boone's book, *A New Song*, which just happened to be on his nightstand. As he read, his eyes were opened. Pat introduced him to the reality of Jesus and the Holy Spirit as a person. He fell on his knees by the bed and opened his heart to Christ.

While he was on his knees, Niqua wandered into the room. "Daddy! What are you doing?"

"I'm praying!" Tears were running down his cheeks.

Dutch spent the rest of the day visiting our pastor and friends, to tell them of his new birth. I was so happy! Praise the Lord!

5

Todd was very fond of Dr. Mikkelson, the urologist. On one of his follow-up visits, Todd took a large picture he had painted to give to him, but to his dismay, Dr. Mikkelson was not there that day. Another doctor walked into the room, and there stood Todd, picture in hand. He didn't want to be impolite and tell the doctor that the picture wasn't for him. What could he do?

With great insight, the doctor offered to make certain that Dr. Mikkelson would receive the picture. A week later, Todd proudly displayed a letter from Dr. Mikkelson:

Dear Todd:

Thank you for the painting. You are quite an artist. We are all pleased that you are recovering so well.

We greatly respected this kind doctor, who took time out from his busy schedule to write a thank-you note to a child.

Todd did crazy things sometimes, perhaps as an attempt to hide his fear, for on these occasions his laughter easily turned to tears. Once, for example, on a visit to the doctor's office, he played around and hid from us. When it was time to leave he ran from room to room, trying to get away from me.

On other occasions he was in such pain that just walking the few steps from the parking lot to the lobby took forever. We couldn't always carry him. Often that would cause more pain. He was most comfortable when he went at his own slow pace, bent over like an old man.

Periodically Todd was readmitted to the hospital. It took quite a while for his stomach pains to subside, which caused us some concern. Also, the chemotherapy suppressed his white blood count, so he was unable to fight infection. A cold could send him to the hospital.

Once his count was so low that the normal germs in the digestive system posed great danger to him. He had violent stomach cramps. He was unable to eat or drink. A drop of water was more than he could handle.

During every hospital stay Todd was tense and afraid until the inevitable IV was started. Then he was ready for action. He would chase

the nurses with his IV pole or visit the playroom for fun and games.

The playroom was always "safe." No shots
were given there, and no examinations except
temperature and blood pressure, which didn't
hurt. Volunteers and parents played games with
the children to occupy and teach them and to
divert attention from their disabilities.

It always amazed me how readily the children accepted one another's illnesses, ban-
dages, and handicaps. No one ever thought of
pointing a finger or making fun. The sight of
another's wound simply triggered compassion.
They all knew what pain was.

The playroom had real blood pressure
gauges, thermometers, and IV equipment (mi-
nus the needle)—all the things the children
were familiar with from the ward. They tried
everything out on dolls, giving them thorough
examinations. Once the children were familiar
with the equipment, they were less afraid when
it came time for it to be used on them.

My mother called in a prayer request for
Todd at a Christian radio station. Several days
later, a host for one of the radio programs and
his wife came to visit Todd at the hospital. A
friendship began when Ron sat on the floor next
to Todd's bed and asked, "Brother, you seem
to know Jesus so well and love him so much.
Will you pray for *me*?"

Then I started hearing the Lord's Prayer again. Over and over I heard it, on the radio, in conversations, in books. One day a friend asked, "Do you know what my favorite Bible verse is?" It was a part of the Lord's Prayer.

Always before, the Lord's Prayer had been a warning of bad news to come. Now each time I heard it I thought, "Oh, no! Not again. Now what?"

In the middle of June, Todd started having pain in his back. At first we thought nothing of it, but every day it became worse. He did not like taking medication, so he just bore the pain.

Even though everyone was watching Todd for any sign of recurring cancer, the doctor thought this probably was a case of shingles. On Friday she suggested we wait to see if he broke out in a rash typical of shingles, and call Monday if there was no change.

All weekend Todd was in pain. The only way he could stand it was sitting straight up. So he tried to sleep nights by sitting in a chair or on the couch, supported by pillows so he would not slouch over. We took turns sleeping next to him in a similar position to help hold him up.

By Monday we were all exhausted from sleepless nights. Todd's pain was worse, and there was no sign of a rash. The doctor suggested we bring him in the following day for tests.

Todd had seemed to be tripping slightly over his own feet. By the time we saw the doctor, he was definitely stumbling. Now the doctor had reason to check for a neurological reason for his back pain.

Todd was admitted to the hospital. I was so frightened, and yet I hoped that now they would finally be able to do something about Todd's pain.

A whole battery of doctors came to check Todd over. But first things first. He had to be hooked up to an IV. That meant more pain, screams, fear, anger.

Neurologists gathered around his bed and examined him by sticking him with a needle-like instrument to determine if he had feeling in his legs and back. By this time he could not walk. He could move his legs, but seemed to have no control over where he placed them. He could not take two steps without falling down.

The doctors talked about Todd as if he weren't there, treating him like an object. He was frightened. He lay with his eyes lowered. I was furious over the doctors' lack of tact and sensitivity, but I didn't have the nerve to speak up.

That night Todd sat in a wheelchair. I tried

45

to get him into bed, but he said that hurt more. A doctor assured me there was no law saying he *had* to go to bed. We walked the halls most of the night.

Todd still hadn't had anything for pain. The doctor ordered it when I asked for it, but by the time the nurse brought it, Todd had gone to sleep. They said not to disturb him, to wait until he woke up. Then the whole procedure was repeated.

They were stalling. They were reluctant to give him anything because of the test scheduled for morning. He would have to be sedated for that.

The test involved taking a small amount of spinal fluid and injecting some dye. The X ray would then show if there was any nerve blockage to account for Todd's loss of feeling in his legs. We were glad Todd was sedated and would feel none of it.

The test seemed to take hours. Dutch and I had trouble trying to pass the time.

When Todd was finally brought to his room, our joy at having him back was short-lived. We were asked to join the doctors for a conference.

What do you do when they tell you they've found more cancer?

Our world caved in again. But God gave us the strength to hear the doctors out. They explained that Todd had a tumor wrapped around his spinal cord. There were only three known cases of Todd's kind of cancer in which this had happened. But that was little consolation to us. Todd would probably soon be paralyzed.

It all happened so fast—too fast to comprehend, too fast to cry. Dutch asked when surgery to remove the tumor would be performed. The surgeon looked at his watch and said, "We're scheduled to begin right away."

There was just time to sign a consent form and try to tell Todd what was happening. He was still sleeping off the anesthesia, but we felt he had to be prepared. Dutch told him to remember that Jesus would be with him. He was too drowsy to hear. They wheeled him from the room.

I finally had time to cry. The doctors were concerned. We knew they hurt with us. Dr. Nelson put his arms around me and assured me that they would do all they could. The surgeon was one of the best.

Then all there was left to do was wait and pray.

I remembered an article in which the writer talked about God's hands being there to minister to our needs. I tried to picture God's hands guiding the surgeon's hands in the delicate operation.

I couldn't stand the long wait, so God allowed me to sleep. He promises that he will not allow us to be tempted beyond that which we are able to endure.

At last they said Todd was out of surgery and would soon be placed in intensive care, where we would be allowed to see him five minutes out of every hour.

I wanted so much to see him, but I was afraid of what he would look like. Before we opened the door, I breathed: "Lord, please help! Come with us. Help us to bear it!"

Todd had tubes attached to him everywhere. His lips were dry and torn. He was pale and didn't know we were there.

Every hour we went in for a few minutes. There were few patients, so we were permitted to stay longer each time.

As drowsiness left Todd, he became frightened and uncomfortable. The pain returned.

At one point he cried out in desperation: "God damn!"

That hurt. It was not like him. But we understood.

Here he had been doing fine. Then the pain came. The last thing he knew, he was having a test. And now he woke up in more pain and tied down by tubes and IVs. He couldn't understand.

The next morning we were called to a conference with the doctors again. You could almost smell the bad news. I didn't want to go,

Todd wanted me to stay with him. But one of the doctors insisted I be there with Dutch. He would stay with Todd.

X rays taken during surgery revealed tumors in Todd's lungs. The disease had spread even more. The hope for Todd's total recovery diminished.

Somehow the news didn't crush us. We went on talking, smiling, feeling, seeing. God was there helping us, shielding us from the blow. There was talk of cobalt treatments and increased chemotherapy. Before we had chosen not to have cobalt treatments, but now we had no choice.

Todd was starting to feel better and we were permitted to spend more time with him. He seemed less uncomfortable than after his first operation. Breathing wasn't as painful, since the incision was on his back. But he was unhappy. He resented having a roommate. He wanted to be alone.

He had to be handled very carefully. The nurses showed me how to "log roll" him, which meant moving him in one motion with the help of a sheet.

We still did not know if he would regain use of his legs completely, but indications were good. The neurological "pricks" showed feeling in his legs. The doctors were pleased.

Then came the day when he could get out

49

of bed again. We resumed our rounds through the halls, with Todd in his wheelchair.

But Todd was depressed. He who could always pray couldn't even be persuaded to say grace.

Then the Lord told me what was wrong. Todd was mad at God! He felt betrayed. He had thought all was well—and now this! He felt guilty for having cursed. He couldn't understand why all this was happening, and he didn't know what to do.

I stopped the wheelchair, turned to him, and said, "You know, Son, it's OK to tell God you're mad at him."

He looked up at me with a smile. A heavy burden had been lifted. "It is?" Later that day he whispered in my ear, "Mom, I've been praying again." He was happy again and soon spent more and more time in the playroom.

He was receiving physical therapy to help him regain the use of his legs. He loved his therapist. He also called several nurses his "special girl friends." He pursued them relentlessly through the halls and waited for their "special tickles." He continued to improve so much that he was discharged a week after surgery.

After the last examination by the neurosurgeon, I wondered how I would be able to take proper care of Todd at home. A small part of his spine was exposed. The doctor smiled and said, "He is *not* going to fall apart."

Todd's physical therapy continued once a week after he was home. He worked hard practicing to walk. He had to concentrate to control the direction his feet went in, and he wobbled a lot.

Once on our daily trips to the hospital for cobalt treatments we met the neurosurgeon in the hall. He was talking on the phone and just pointed to Todd in amazement as he walked by. He obviously had not expected such progress.

Since the tumor had been wrapped around the spinal cord, the doctors could not be sure they had removed all of it. The cobalt treatments were directed at the spine and would eventually weaken it. We were told that, should Todd live to be a teenager, we could then expect problems with his back. They advised us to try to direct his interests away from anything that would strain his back. But we really had no choice about the radiation. The prospect of possible back trouble years in the future did not weigh as heavily as the immediate danger of cancer.

Swimming was good exercise for him, so I took him to the YWCA. They let him use the pool, but the lifeguard eyed him with great concern. His back was marked with a green

51

marker to show the area of radiation. He did look weird. But he had fun.

When chemotherapy was resumed, the potent drug caused all Todd's hair to fall out. The object of chemotherapy is to kill fast-growing cells, because cancer cells grow fast. Since hair cells also grow fast, chemotherapy killed them as well.

His hair was all over his pillow at night. It was in his mouth. It fell in his food when he ate. His comb brought out bushels of hair. It was like combing a shedding dog. After a few days of this, we had a talk with Todd and he agreed to have his hair cut very short so it wouldn't bother him so much when it fell out.

He was embarrassed about it, though, and from then on he usually wore his baseball cap. But he always saw other kids at the hospital who were just as bald as he was.

Pastor and Mrs. Roufs came to see him again. They brought prayers, gifts, and encouragement, and a verse of Scripture: "Is any among you sick? Let him call for the elders of the church, and let them pray over him, anointing him with oil in the name of the Lord; and the prayer of faith will save the sick man, and the Lord will raise him up; and if he has committed sins, he will be forgiven" (James 5:14).

Pastor Roufs suggested that we might call the elders and that he would anoint Todd with oil. But he said it was up to us, and we had to decide and initiate it. It sounded OK to us, but we didn't follow through on it. I suppose we just weren't ready.

I read in the paper that a boy who had been in a hospital room next to Todd's had died. The paper also told of the Christian testimony his mother had given at the funeral.

I thought then that if a woman's child died, her world must stop turning and the sun must stop shining, and she would walk around in a veil of tears and shock. But to see that boy's mother at the hospital the day after the funeral, beaming and testifying to the love of God, was almost disturbing.

She told me she had asked for an altar call at the funeral. "You didn't!" I said. "You couldn't have!"

"Of course! What better time is there?" she asked. "At no other time are people as aware and open and receptive as at a funeral. It was perfect. And I think someone received the Lord that day."

It was hard for me to understand, but a seed was sown in my heart.

Todd was in and out of the hospital. The tumors in his lungs were growing, so his chemotherapy was in heavy doses, and he sometimes had reactions to it. When his white blood count was too low, he had to be admitted to the hospital. At this point a cold could have killed him.

We were very fond of Dr. Nelson, Todd's hematologist. We talked to him over lunch one day of our struggles and our faith in God. I told him how I had often felt like shaking him and picking his brain for any advice, any hope, *anything*. We always wondered if there was anything else in the world we could do for Todd, anywhere else we could take him. Did someone else have more knowledge, different treatments? Perhaps the doctors in Mexico or on the moon had a better idea.

Dr. Nelson had tears in his eyes as we told him that now we had placed Todd in God's hands. We told him we were trusting God to give the doctors wisdom, and that we would agree to anything Dr. Nelson suggested.

Dr. Nelson admitted humbly that wisdom did not come from him, but from higher up. We felt a special bond of closeness with him.

Some weeks later Dr. Nelson took time from his busy schedule to sit on the couch of Todd's hospital room with me and talk about our hopes and dreams for the present and the future. I dared ask him then how much longer he thought Todd might have to live.

"Perhaps six months."

6

Todd decided he wanted to learn to run again. I pleaded with him to practice on the grass so he wouldn't hurt himself when he fell. He wobbled down our small stretch of grass faster and faster each day until his wobble almost resembled a run. We watched with joy at his determination, but with sadness at seeing him so disabled.

He began pitching baseball. Someone had given him a "pitchback" as a gift. He was good. I laughed at the funny faces he made during the windup, but he assured me that was all part of it.

I wanted to protect Todd and wrap him in cotton so he wouldn't hurt himself. But praise

God, he gave us the sense to let Todd be as normal a boy as he could be.

Sunday was going to be a picture-taking day at Dodger Stadium in Los Angeles. The thought of having his picture taken with Ron Cey made Todd's head swim. We borrowed a camera we thought would work better than our own, to be sure we would get good pictures. I even planned to go, though I've never been a baseball fan.

But when Sunday came, Todd was sick. He had a temperature, and he was so weak he could hardly stand. He pleaded with us to take him anyway. He was determined we would not keep him home.

We carried our little bundle of skin and bones and supported him between us. He was so weak. A woman next to us asked me why Todd looked so ill. She bought him a flag and prayed for him. Later she wrote to him and sent him get-well cards from children in her neighborhood, along with gifts of money and many more prayers.

Todd did have his picture taken with several of his favorite players. He watched several innings before he admitted that he was too sick to stay any longer.

His temperature was high and his breathing heavy by the time we got home. We put him to bed, and in his sleep he almost seemed unconscious. We wrung our hands and wondered what to do. Clearly we should take him to the hospital, but he was so sick, we feared we would never bring him home again. We didn't want to take that final step yet.

But we had to do something. Dutch decided to go to the home of friends and ask them to pray with him. Maybe they would know what we should do.

I sat next to Todd, holding his hand and crying. His fever was high, and he seemed delirious. He was talking in his sleep. Fear gripped me. I had never met death in any form. What if Todd died now while I was alone with him?

Then I remembered someone telling me that the Bible says God will wipe away all our tears in heaven. My tears stopped. I couldn't think of any reason to be crying. And suddenly Todd opened his eyes, looked around, smiled, and said: "Has anyone been praying for me?"

"Oh yes, Son, yes!" I rushed to the phone to tell Dutch. He had been praying for Todd with our friends. He said the Lord seemed to be directing them to go to a worship service that same night at the Church on the Way in Van Nuys.

We dressed Todd and Dutch carried him into the church just as the service began. We sat in the very last row in an overflow crowd. Then

Todd got a nosebleed, the worst he had ever had. Three elders invited us to a basement room, where they worked with Todd, trying to stop the bleeding. At one point, when they removed the tissue from Todd's nose, they pulled out a blood clot several inches long. No matter what they did, the bleeding did not stop.

The elders asked permission to anoint Todd with oil. We gave it gladly as we huddled on the floor around him. As they prayed, I thought that if Todd had to die this would be a perfect time. Peace came over me.

As soon as they had prayed, the bleeding stopped. I remembered the Bible story of Peter walking on the water to meet his Lord. "When he saw the wind, he was afraid, and beginning to sink he cried out, 'Lord, save me.' Jesus immediately reached out his hand and caught him, saying to him, 'O man of little faith, why did you doubt?' "

I drew strength from that lesson many times. When the storm howled against us and we feared we would sink into the waves, we cried, "Lord, save me!" And he did.

The next day Todd had improved so much, it was hard to believe he had been so sick. But he had low-grade pneumonia and was admitted to the hospital. Again I moved in with him.

I almost enjoyed the hospital stays. They offered us time to pray, both for ourselves and for others. Todd and I would walk the halls, wondering whom God wanted us to pray for this time.

Todd always wondered who his intern would be. By now he knew who was gentle and who wasn't. Some were so careful in starting an IV, even offering to use a smaller needle. Others were not so gentle. It was hard to find one small vein in an arm that had been stuck so many times before.

Once Todd was assigned a doctor who was obviously not feeling well himself. Todd's veins were hard to find, and the doctor had to try four times before the IV was in.

Todd had given up fighting the needle and just lay there whimpering. "Man, doctor, you better go to school and learn how to do this," he said.

"I've been to school already," the doctor mumbled.

"Well, you better go back some more!" They never did become friends.

At first I would stay with Todd when he needed an injection, hoping I could calm him down and persuade him to hold still. Or I would help the nurse hold him down. Sometimes he screamed so much that his face became red and he was wet from perspiration. Then all I could do was leave the room and promise to return as soon as he calmed down.

Dutch tried to help too. He spent much time trying to give Todd courage, explaining the treatments, offering Todd rewards if he would hold still, wiping Todd's tears as Todd clenched his teeth, trying to obey. Todd knew the procedure was easier when he held still, but his fear of the needle was usually stronger than that knowledge. My heart ached for him, and I felt like screaming and crying myself.

But once the needle was in, Todd was usually free to chase the nurse or go to the playroom and participate in one of the many planned activities. There was even a teacher on the floor. She had a little room filled with school materials, and she came and taught each child individually.

The doctors tried various drugs to combat Todd's cancer. One would show results for a time. Then his natural antibodies would combat the drug and it would lose its effectiveness, so a new one would have to be tried. One doctor gave up some of his weekends to evaluate Todd's X rays, trying to determine the failure or success of the chemicals.

Many times we hoped a certain combination would hold the cancer cells back. Whenever Todd started losing ground, the doctors switched to a new combination. With each drug that failed, there were fewer left to try.

Dr. Nelson asked if we might give permission for an experiment. It involved adding a certain amount of radium to a drug and then taking a series of blood tests to determine the effectiveness. The tests probably would not help Todd because the results would take time to evaluate, and the procedure called for two IVs, one in each arm. But Todd agreed to give it a try, since it might help someone else sometime.

The day before the test we were told that Dutch had a spot on his lung. That news loomed as another threat, since it, too, could mean cancer. But we were still trusting God.

Billy Graham was in town for a crusade and we were looking forward to joining others from our church to hear him at the Hollywood Bowl.

About noon, some lab technicians came to Todd's room for a blood sample. They took us completely by surprise. Todd had already had his routine blood test early in the morning. We were usually informed ahead of time when a test was ordered, but we didn't know anything about this one. The technician was inexperienced, and I could feel my blood pressure rising.

I ran out of the room and into the doctor's office, where our intern was eating lunch. "Who ordered a blood test on Todd?" I demanded. The intern said that she had. They needed it to be able to evaluate the results of the test the next day. She had assumed it had been explained to me.

"Well, they're in there now and Todd is fighting them and I think I'm getting hysterical. You better get in there and help!"

The intern dropped her french fries and ran to Todd's room. The commotion attracted other nurses, and soon the room was full of people, all trying to get blood from Todd. I started to cry and couldn't stop.

A nurse took me to a conference room to try to calm me down. I withdrew permission for the test the next day. I told her I did not want *anyone* touching Todd anymore until my husband got there. I called Dutch and asked him to come right away.

Between sobs, I tried to explain to the nurse that I had helped hold Todd down for many procedures when I knew they were necessary, but this time the test was voluntary, and I could stand seeing Todd screaming and crying *no more!* The nurse promised that Todd would be left alone until Dutch came.

My nerves had given way and all my pain came out in a flood of sobbing. I lay on the couch in Todd's room and cried. Doctors and nurses came to try to console me. They offered to bring me aspirin and to rub my neck, for by now I had a splitting headache.

Finally Todd said, "Mom, would you like

me to pray for you?" He took hold of my hand, bowed his little bald head, and said, "Dear Jesus, please help my mom."

Dutch came and we met with Dr. Nelson. Again I explained how I could stand almost anything if it had to be, but I could not stand this. He was so understanding. We could tell that he sympathized with us.

We agreed to give it one try the next day. If a vein could not be found on the first try, the whole test would be called off, and should the IV infiltrate or clog, the test would be discontinued.

I was physically and emotionally drained, and the prospect of leaving Todd to go to the crusade wasn't inviting anymore. Dutch insisted that I go with him: "You need to get out of here for a while." The intern promised to do paperwork in Todd's room to keep him company.

Seeing all our friends and our pastor was comforting, but I still couldn't hold back the tears. I was sobbing again before we left for the Hollywood Bowl. One friend tried to console me as I told her what had happened that day. Others just wondered and prayed for us.

The crusade choir sang "Because he lives I can face tomorrow," and my pain was soothed. I knew Jesus was there, enfolding me with his love. He would not leave us. God had promised that he would not allow us to be tempted beyond that which we could endure. He would provide a way of escape.

It was late when Dutch brought me back to the hospital. He understood that I wanted to be with Todd. I found him sound asleep, with the radio softly playing hymns. The nurses told me my sister had been with him and kept him company until he went to sleep.

I was exhausted, but I felt the urge to go and have a cup of coffee. In the waiting room I found a woman sitting stiffly on the couch. I went over to her and asked if there was anything I could do for her. She looked at me and burst out, "What can you do for me when my son is dying?"

Oh, I knew how she felt. I tried to point her to Jesus, who I knew would help her as he helped me. We talked and talked, yet she was bitter. "How could God allow this? You sound just like that chaplain at the last hospital we were at." But at least she did lie down on the couch in their room for a while. She hadn't slept for days.

About 3:00 in the morning, I finally went to sleep. Yes, because he lives, I could face tomorrow.

The woman whose son was dying continued in her pain. She bore the burden of all the decisions and all the sorrow herself. She fought with the doctors. "Dammit, doctor, I hate your guts, but you're the only chance my son has got." She had put her trust in medicine, and it failed her.

Todd's test the next day went fine, and the spot on Dutch's lung later proved to be harmless.

7

Disneyland, here we come!

Todd had been to Disneyland when he was very small, and he didn't remember it. Niqua had never been there. We planned a great day.

Mickey Mouse and Robin Hood and Little John were there, and the children said hi to them. Robin Hood grabbed Todd's baseball cap off his head, and we have pictures of Todd looking around to see who took it and of his happy smile when Robin gave it back.

Dutch and Todd rode the Matterhorn, and we all rode the train around to different "lands." There was so much to do, so much to see, we hardly had time for lunch!

Todd's seventh birthday found us at the Los

Angeles Zoo. We invited all his friends to come with us and had a picnic with all the trimmings.

Todd wasn't feeling very well, and we were concerned that we may have planned too much for him. My emotions were mixed that day. It was wonderful to share the children's joy as they watched the different animals. What an experience it was for their inquisitive minds. Yet I kept asking myself, "What if this is his last birthday with us?" How could I bear the thought?

Faith! The word seemed to leap out at me from the pages of the Bible:

"According to your faith be it done to you."

"Your faith has made you well."

"He said to them, 'Where is your faith?' "

"If you have faith as a grain of mustard seed. . . ."

Faith! I needed it—lots of it. And if Todd was to have a miracle healing, I didn't have years to grow in faith. I needed it now.

"What if I don't come up with enough faith?" I asked myself. "If I don't come up with enough faith, Todd is going to die! And it will be my fault!" I felt a trap closing tighter.

"Our Father, who art in heaven, hallowed be thy name. Thy kingdom come, thy will be done. . . ." I needed to give up my will for Todd and pray that God's will be done, even if that meant God would take Todd.

Our hopes and fears during this time are reflected in a letter I wrote to Dutch's parents:

Duane is taking it better than I am. I have talked so much about children being gifts of God and not possessions, but it sure does test your faith when it comes right down to it. We want to hang on. We do think that Todd would be better off if he could die. It's just that we are so selfish and human we want him to live. Isn't it great to know that if he dies, he will go to heaven?

Todd is such a good boy. In his last report card he had 10 Es for excellent. And he deserved them. Whatever he does, he has to give it his best. Perhaps he is too good for this world and the Lord is calling him home early. We'll know someday.

Todd has his own ministry. People halfway around the world are praying for him, and nonchristians are watching to see how our faith helps us through this.

Friends, too, were hit by the shock waves of this illness. One couple cried out to God in a prayer which they lovingly presented to us:

A Prayer for Toddy
by John and Kathy
Dear heavenly Father, Toddy is very sick, and no one here knows what to do about it. He is such a little guy for an illness so drastic, and we are all too weak to

accept what is happening to him. We love him so much.

It seems unfair to you that we pray in time of need, but I think you know that our hearts are with you always, and you are the power, the love, and the way for all of us.

It also seems unfair for such a little boy of six not to have the chance to enjoy the life you gave him.

We are human and do not understand your way sometimes. If Toddy has almost completed his mission on this earth, he must be very strong, very beautiful, very blessed, and very much a needed soul in your work up there.

If that's the case, grant us the strength to accept it and always take care of him for us. But if there is some way he can help you and still remain with us, please, please, help him overcome this illness. He brings so much love, so much joy, and so much kindness to us. We need him.

One once said that faith moves mountains. We may lose everything but faith in your wisdom and decisions, because we know that you want the best for Toddy as well as we do.

We say these things to you in the name of Jesus Christ, who gloriously completed his mission on this earth and returned to you for greater love. Amen.

Still there were times when we cried, "Why, God? Why Todd? Why us? Why the anguish? Why the suffering?" Then the Holy Spirit led us to Hebrews 12:

> Consider him who endured from sinners such hostility against himself, so that you may not grow weary or fainthearted. In your struggle against sin you have not yet resisted to the point of shedding your blood. And have you forgotten the exhortation which addresses you as sons?—"My son, do not regard lightly the discipline of the Lord, nor lose courage when you are punished by him. For the Lord disciplines him whom he loves, and chastises every son whom he receives." It is for discipline that you have to endure. God is treating you as sons; for what son is there whom his father does not discipline? . . . For the moment all discipline seems painful rather than pleasant; later it yields the peaceful fruit of righteousness to those who have been trained by it.

One night I dreamed that I handed Todd over to the Lord. The dream was so vivid that I almost felt the weight of Todd's body on my arms. And Jesus accepted him. After that I felt relief. Todd was the Lord's responsibility. He would care for him.

My desperate search for adequate faith gave

71

way to trust in the perfect will of God. The Lord supplied simple faith like that of the leper in Matthew 8:3: " 'Lord, if you will, you can make me clean.' And he stretched out his hand and touched him, saying, 'I will; be clean.' "

Now I could praise God when the news was bad and even confess to him my unbelief. It was his mercy that would save Todd, and he would supply the faith we needed. Now my vision was again clear, and I looked to the Giver rather than the gift.

8

"We have run out of all the known agents that have any effect in cases like Todd's. But we do have one drug left that we'd like to try. It has been used for leukemia, but never with solid tumors. It has the advantage of being in tablet form, so we wouldn't have to inject it into the bloodstream."

We decided to try it. The doctor told us to give Todd three tablets each morning. But when we had the prescription filled, the instructions read: "One tablet in the morning." We thought we had misunderstood the doctor. So for a week, Todd forced one pill down every morning.

But at our next clinic visit the X rays harbored bad news. The tumors in his lungs had spread a great deal. He had one large one and four or more small ones. The large one was about the size of a fist. They were growing at a fast rate.

Dr. Nelson told us there was no more hope. Obviously the drug had not worked, and there were no more to try. He suggested we take Todd home and keep him as comfortable as we could.

Later we learned that Dr. Nelson was crying as he left us.

The news was devastating—yet all I could think was, "Praise God from whom all blessings flow."

We had met some parents who had taken their little daughter home to die. The mother had learned to give morphine injections. I wanted to learn to give injections so we could keep Todd at home to the end. I thought it might be nicer that way, but Dutch didn't: "I can't think of anything nice about it!"

Then we discovered the mistaken dosage. Dr. Nelson thought we should try again, using the correct dosage, just so we would never look back and say, "What if . . .?"

Our friends at church organized a 24-hour prayer vigil. On September 28, people stopped during the day and got up at all hours of the night to join in prayer for Todd. We felt enfolded by the love of God that day, and we

74

were comforted, knowing someone was praying every moment.

A letter to Dutch's parents tells what happened:

It's hard to put into words all of what we are learning and experiencing. When they prayed for Todd that whole day, it completely changed the congregation. One woman told me today that the Lord is drawing everyone together, using Todd as the link. When we walk down the aisle now on Sundays, it's as if we had come to a family thanksgiving gathering. You can feel the love of the people, not only for us but for each other.

I know the Lord is using Todd for his glory. Many people have reevaluated their lives and their relationship to God because of what we are going through. Everyone woke up; they have been touched where they hurt too and they can see firsthand how the Lord gives us strength. If Todd's suffering will result in just one person drawn to the Lord and helped, it will be worth it.

I've been talking to Todd about completely turning his life over to Jesus and following his leading. He wants to know if many other people have done that and if we're going to do it. I told him that when he is ready all he has to do is pray about

it the same way he did when he asked
Jesus into his heart. He thinks about death
and going to heaven a lot—not with fear,
but with confidence. He is just curious
what it is going to be like.

On the Sunday after Dr. Nelson had told us
to take Todd home, Pastor Roufs anointed
Todd with oil during both services and the
congregation joined with us again in prayer for
Todd according to the admonition in James
5:14-15.

Our faith was very small that day. "O God, I
believe, help thou my unbelief." But the people
of the church joined their faith to ours. We felt
the love of God through his body, the church.
They felt compassion and they opened their
hearts and prayed for us.

It was as if we could reach out and touch the
love that was flowing to us from the people.
They were crying for us and with us, praying
for us and giving of their inner selves. We were
no longer strangers. Now we were one family,
one body. One member of the body hurt, and
the other members rushed to its aid.

If Todd could walk, he was in church. We
heard that his being there was an inspiration to
other children. They said, "If Todd can make it
to church, then so can I." Todd listened to the
sermons and turned to the songs, singing along

when he could. As the tumors grew in his lungs, he no longer had breath enough to sing.

Going up to the altar with us when we received Communion, the children were blessed by the laying on of hands as an act of worship for Todd. Sometimes he would stand next to the pastor after the service and shake hands with people as they left.

At Todd's first clinic visit since we'd corrected the dosage of his medicine, we went through the usual routine. First came the blood test at the lab. By now the technicians had come to know Todd. They were good at their jobs and seemed to be able to find veins even better than the doctors. Todd fought them at first, but gradually he learned to trust them. He wouldn't scream and kick, but he played endless games and tricks on them before finally settling down for the procedure.

After the blood test came a visit to the X-ray department so the doctors could check the rate of growth of the tumors. The X ray didn't hurt, so Todd relaxed. Here he had friends, and when he felt good he would joke and giggle with the nurses.

Next we usually went to the cafeteria for lunch or stopped by the hospital to say hi to the nurses and doctors and to the other kids and their parents. My standard questions to the nurses were: "Who is here? How is . . . ?"

At 12:45 we would sign up in the clinic and wait for the nurse to call Todd into the prep room to take his temperature and weigh and measure him. The wait then continued until the doctors arrived. That was the routine.

So it was that day. We were still waiting for a room. Todd was running around the halls, giggling and laughing and playing tricks on the nurses. At one point he crawled under a nurse's cart to hide.

The doctors arrived, took one look at Todd, and left again.

Later they told us that when they saw Todd running around they knew something must have happened and they wanted to see the X rays. So they hurried back down to the X-ray department before even seeing Todd.

The tumors had shrunk considerably! It was a miracle!

The next week the doctor told us that another doctor from radiology had called him and asked what treatment they were using, because he had never seen anything like it. "Whatever you're doing, don't quit!" We were elated.

The tumors steadily receded. When we got home Monday evenings after clinic, the phone would start ringing, with people asking, "How much did the tumors go down?" The answer was better each time: 50%, 60%—then 90%!

One day the doctor from radiology asked to

see me urgently. He banged the X rays into the visor to show me the "before and after." At least five tumors had been reduced to one-tenth of their original size. Praise God!

And we were praising God. I seemed to have a compulsion to proclaim the miracle. I felt I was denying him if I let any occasion go by without telling what God had done for us.

One day, when I was on the phone, telling for the umpteenth time how much the tumors had shrunk and that the doctors said it was a miracle, Dutch said, "You're going to scream if you have to tell it one more time. Let it be."

"What do you mean? God performed a miracle! We have to tell!"

But then I realized how weary I was. Satan had turned our joy into a burden. After that I relaxed. My compulsion to tell was replaced with quietness. I knew God would provide the opportunity when he wanted the story told.

Todd, too had been busy proclaiming his miracle. He called in to a Christian radio station and a program host spoke with him on the air. Here is part of their conversation:

Host: Todd here—he was a pretty sick boy. He had tumors all through his insides. His grandmother wrote me over here at the radio station about six months ago and mentioned about Todd and sent a picture along, and we began to pray for him and a lot of the people listening I'm sure were praying. And I think we got a phone call one day, too, and we realized that you were in the hospital there. And I decided to come over and see you and there you were. And we've been good friends ever since then. Right, Todd?

Todd: Right.

Host: And can you tell the people some of the things that happened since then? You're not so sick anymore. Right?

Todd: No.

Host: What happened?

Todd: It started out with a tumor wrapped around one of my kidneys. And we took that kidney out. And then there was some wrapped around my spine. That was the second surgery I had.

Host: Aha. And so they took some of those tumors out, right?

Todd: Right.

Host: What happened to the rest of them?

Todd: The rest? One of them went all the way down and one is almost gone and we don't know about the rest.

Host: But some of these tumors are going away. And nobody's operated on them or anything?

Todd: No.

Host: That's fantastic. And I know you're

pretty happy about it. 'Cause you've been going to school since then, haven't you?

Todd: Yeah.

Host: What grade are you in?

Todd: Second.

Host: Second. That's really good. Hey, I want to ask you this.

Todd: Yeah?

Host: Do you love Jesus?

Todd: Yeah.

Host: Why?

Todd: Because he healed me and he gave us everything.

Host: Are you looking forward to seeing Jesus pretty soon?

Todd: Yeah.

Host: Hey, Todd, I appreciate your sharing a little bit with us today of what's happened to you. And we're just going to keep on praying that the Lord continues to do this healing process. You want to say anything for the people?

Todd: Since you helped pray for me, just call me and I'll pray for you.

Host: Sounds fair enough. Thanks, Todd. God bless you.

At the hospital, when we described our miracle to other parents, I sensed a wall go up between us. We had seen that wall in different stages of construction in front of most parents at the hospital. We were even busy erecting one ourselves. It was made up of: "You don't understand! You're not going through what I'm going through. Where do you come off giving me advice? You don't hurt like I hurt. My cross is heavier than yours."

Some did rejoice with us over Todd's apparent recovery, but I could see the pain the others felt over their own loss. It seemed that while Todd was getting worse I could speak with authority to other mothers about God's help in trouble. I *knew* what they were going through. But when Todd was better, there was that wall.

One of Todd's friends at the hospital was close to death. We stopped in often to ask how he was.

We had bought a series of colorful pictures showing Jesus during his ministry. The one that impressed Todd most showed Lazarus as he walked from his tomb. Todd wrote alongside the picture: "This is when God changed his mind." He delivered the picture to his friend's mother to encourage her that God might change his mind about taking her son.

Then one day the nurses told me the boy had died. I didn't tell Todd. He had prayed that Jesus would change his mind, and now I didn't know what to say to him.

The following Friday he had to go in for a blood test. My brother Tom took him, and afterward they went visiting. Todd didn't talk much all day, but that night he asked, "Mom, did Gregg die?"

"Yes, son, he did."

"I thought so," he said. "When I was up there today someone else was in his room. . . . Mom, if you leave your body here when you go to heaven, how do people know that you're gone? Do you take your bones with you? How about your heart?" He giggled. "If you get a new body in heaven and you take your old heart, then you would have two hearts—one for Jesus to come into and one for God to come into." He thought that was neat. "Mom, if you don't take your eyes with you to heaven, then how are you going to see Jesus?"

We had many more talks about heaven. He felt that my mother should come with him. "Hold up your hands next to mine," he said to her. "Let me see if they got any smaller yet. You're going to have to hurry up and shrink if you're going to go to heaven with me."

In his Bible was a picture of Jesus and some children playing near water. "Goody! There's going to be a beach in heaven!"

Todd loved to go to Forest Lawn Cemetery, to see all the statues and to watch the presentation of the crucifixion and resurrection paintings. My mother took the kids as often as she could. They would start off by the little lake with ducks, and then go to Babyland and embrace the statue of a baby with outstretched arms. They would look up to the statue of Christ in awe.

More and more I started wondering about the time "after"—if Todd was going to die. Even though we never talked about it, I assumed he would be buried at Forest Lawn. The cemetery is situated on a hill, visible from all over our area. I wondered how I would be able to stand the sight of it, knowing my son was buried there.

On our next clinic visit, the nurse and psychiatrist called me out of the waiting room into an office. I half expected them to question me about Todd's healing. But the little conference was not about our miracle. They told me our beloved Dr. Nelson had suffered a stroke. He had not regained consciousness, and the situation looked grave. I was so sorry, but I had no doubt that he would recover. It seemed ironic that the last time I talked to him he was crying because he thought Todd only had two weeks left to live.

I knew from previous talks with other parents that a change in physician posed a great threat to them. They placed all their trust in a person: the doctor. Now, even if Dr. Nelson recovered, it would be some time before he would be seeing patients again, so we had to be assigned to a new doctor. But we had placed Todd in God's hands, not the doctor's. Dr. Nelson was one of the best. But just as we had prayed for wisdom for Dr. Nelson, so we would pray for wisdom for whatever doctor they assigned to us. Todd took the news quite well and started praying for Dr. Nelson.

The news spread through the hospital. "Did you hear about Dr. Nelson?" There was shock. Everyone was confronted with the fact that doctors get sick and die too. We had built them up almost as gods.

A few days later Dr. Nelson passed away. Only 42 years old, he had been one of the pioneers of chemotherapy. He was our ally in the battle against cancer, and our friend.

I thought we had become quite calloused against death and dying. We were confronted with it so much that it had become part of our lives. But we grieved for the loss of Dr. Nelson, and gratefully remembered the times of fellowship we'd had with him.

9

Todd was back in school. He thought his teacher was one of the nicest people he knew. He was eager to learn and participate, and proud of every accomplishment.

At home, he practiced baseball by the hour in our backyard. He wanted so much to participate in ball games at school, but his running was merely a fast wobble. The kids and teacher would give him a chance, but his frustration at not being able to play as the others was obvious.

Once at a church picnic he got right in there and swung a bat. He was so proud when he hit the ball. He tried to run as fast as he could. It seemed so unfair that he couldn't run like the other kids. But if he felt cheated, it did not keep him from trying.

It was a battle every morning to get him to take those large, bad-tasting pills. We dreaded the ordeal. He couldn't swallow them, so he chewed them. He would chew and gag. If he threw them up we had to start all over again, so he tried to keep them down by breathing deeply. Many mornings ended in tears, with puddles to clean.

Dutch was always thinking of new ways to help Todd take those pills. Our hearts were breaking and our stomachs churning as we watched him gag. How I wished we could stop that medication. "O God, why don't you heal him without those dreadful pills?"

So by the time Todd would leave for school, he had had quite a session already. I was reluctant to let him go. He might get sick in school from the medication. He might be too weak.

Sending him to school also involved the risk of infection, and I found that I was jealous of the time I was not with him. We felt that our days together were numbered, so time was precious. But Todd had all the typical boy's desires and hopes and drives. When he was feeling halfway fine, he wanted to be in school. We realized that we could not deprive him of that.

I brought him his lunch every day instead of

sending it with him, so I had an excuse to check up on him and take him home if necessary. But not matter how he felt, he usually succeeded in talking me into letting him stay for the remainder of the day. Of course, the teacher watched him closely also and would call me if she noticed he'd had enough.

Each week Todd had a blood test. The white count would determine if he was to have any chemotherapy that week. If it was fair, he would have to take the pills, so we naturally hoped for it to be low. But a low count and subsequent interruption of the therapy meant the cancer cells were probably growing. His resistance would be so low that a cold could kill him, and the natural bacteria within his own body posed a threat.

Todd's fondest hope was to become a fire fighter. One late night we were sitting in the waiting room of the X-ray department. Todd had chest pains and we were trying to determine if it was just the tumors or if he had pneumonia. Suddenly a fire alarm sounded, and soon after, to Todd's delight, there were fire fighters running in and out, checking for the cause for the alarm. They never did find any fire, but for Todd, the hospital stay was worthwhile, since he got to see those fire fighters in action. And to think, one of them even came over and talked to him!

At times we were tempted to neglect Todd's discipline. It seemed harsh to discipline a child when he was suffering so much already, but by the grace of God we usually avoided that trap. Now more than ever, Todd needed our guidance and a clear knowledge of right and wrong. He needed to know that we loved him too much to let him grow up to be a bad boy. If we had let him get by with things he might have thought we didn't care, and our lack of discipline would have indicated that we thought he was dying.

One night Todd was cross and refused to go to bed. When I insisted he go, he began to pout and cry. Finally he shouted, "I wish I were already dead!"

That hurt so much, I just turned and went to the living room and knelt in front of my chair and sobbed. After a while Todd came and apologized and we cried together. He was sorry. We talked about how growing up meant learning to listen. Niqua joined us and the three of us huddled together and had a good cry.

God showed us that the quantity of time mattered less than the quality of time we spent together. We got to know Todd better during his illess than we might have known him during a "whole" lifetime. We were allies in battle. We were a shield between him and pain. Together we learned to walk with Jesus. Together we learned compassion for those who hurt. Together we learned to pray for those who did not know of the love of Jesus. We shared our pain and our victories with each other and with Jesus. We could not wrap Todd in cotton and protect him from everything, so we committed him to the Lord.

I kept talking to Todd about making Jesus Lord of his life, to promise to follow wherever Jesus would lead. He thought it through for quite a while. Every week or so, I would ask him, "Have you made up your mind?"

Children create a treasure of little notes and pictures. The ones we have saved from Todd reflect his deep concern that others should not be hurting the way he was, and also his love for Jesus.

"Not yet."

But then one day he had.

"Well, I guess whatever Jesus wants me to do is OK with me. Even if I can't be a fireman. I'll be a pastor if that's what Jesus wants."

When Halloween came, Todd wanted to go trick-or-treating. We weren't sure he could manage the walking, since the slightest stress would leave him gasping for air. But he was determined not to have that ruin his fun. We made our way slowly from house to house, stopping often so he could catch his breath. I was proud at his determination, but his breathless "Trick or Treat" brought tears to my eyes.

For Thanksgiving friends offered to share with us a weekend vacation home they had rented. We accepted gratefully. Todd's tumors were receding by then and he was feeling better and able to do more things. He looked forward to playing in the snow. His excitement is reflected in a letter he wrote to his brother John in Iowa.

We had many days of depression and near desperation. A freak phone call upset my day. A solicitor from a mortuary called encouraging me to prepare. It was a canvass call so he had no knowledge of our situation, but I almost shouted at him. I said I wasn't ready to make such preparations. He chuckled and said something about my not thinking that I was "that

Dear John

I wish you could come to Mamouth with us. Snow is going to be rite in front of are door. I hope you are doine good work in school. Whin you were here you was a good brother. God Loves you. I hope you will have a good Christmas. I hope you will have a good present this Christmas.

Love Todd

old" yet. I wanted to yell at him that my son wasn't "that old." All my bitterness over Todd's illness welled up and I wanted to hurl it at the caller, but I simply hung up.

The next day a friend came to visit and to take my order for Christmas cards. I needed to decide how to have the cards inscribed. Would Todd still be with us by Christmas? Should the cards include his name? It seems a trivial matter now, but then I started sobbing.

Often I found comfort in God's Word, and in words set to music from the hearts of his people. The songs Dale Evans and Roy Rogers sang brought special comfort. They had lost several children. They knew.

One day at the hospital I stopped in the retreat room reserved for parents. This poem was framed on the wall:

TO ALL PARENTS

"I will lend you, for a little time,
A child of mine," He said,
"For you to love the while he lives,
And mourn for when he's dead.

It may be six or seven years,
Or twenty-two or three
But will you, till I call him back,
Take care of him for Me?

He'll bring his charms to gladden you,
And should his stay be brief,
You'll have his lovely memories
As solace for your grief.

I cannot promise he will stay
Since all from earth return,
But there are lessons taught down there
I want this child to learn.

I've looked the wide world over,
In search for teachers true,
And from the throngs that crowd life's lanes
I have selected you.

Now will you give him all your love,
Nor think the labor vain,
Nor hate me when I come to call
To take him back again?

I fancied that I heard them say,
'Dear Lord, Thy will be done!
For all the joys Thy child shall bring
The risk of grief we'll run.

We'll shelter him with tenderness,
We'll love him while we may,
And for the happiness we've known,
Forever grateful stay.

But should the angels call for him
Much sooner than we've planned,
We'll brave the bitter grief that comes
And try to understand.' "

—Edgar Guest

Oh, how it hurt to read that. I could hardly
bear to read the last verse, and yet, already it
was giving me strength. I determined that, if
Todd should die, the poem would be handed
to all at the funeral.

Dutch and I were teaching Sunday school as regularly as we could. He had a class of teenagers who seemed to respond to him and to the message of Christ, as Dutch opened up our lives to them and shared the reality of Christ as we knew it.

I helped in Todd's class. He enjoyed having me as one of his teachers, and I treasured sharing with the children. I prayed with them and encouraged them to talk to Jesus.

Once Pastor Roufs asked if I would have the opening prayer at a Sunday school teachers' meeting. I'm sure he had in mind a few simple words, but when I got up, my heart was so full of the events of the day that the prayer turned into a sermon.

I'd been at the hospital with Todd that day. Todd's roommate Ross had leukemia. I had talked to his mother and learned that they too knew and loved Jesus. She stayed with Ross as much as possible and was always there when any treatment was planned. But that day Ross was alone when the doctor decided he needed a blood transfusion. Ross was usually quiet and he never complained, but now he was terrified. An IV! And his mother was not there! He cried and cried and fought all the efforts to start the IV.

Finally I put my arm around him and asked, "Ross, you know Jesus, don't you?"

He nodded. "Yes."

"Well, Jesus promised that he would *never* leave you. That means he's with you right now and will help you while they start the IV."

Ross dried up his tears, lay down on the bed, and allowed them to try for a vein. He was still crying softly, but the panic was gone. Jesus was there.

I told the Sunday school teachers about Ross, and I said that if they got nothing else through to the children, they must introduce them to Jesus so he would be as close to them in their daily lives as he was to Ross that day. "For some children, time may be running out," I said. "Tell them about Jesus *now*."

10

We hardly allowed ourselves to wonder if this would be Todd's last Christmas with us. He was so excited. To think that Christmas was Jesus' birthday! On every possible occasion in prayer, he giggled and wished Jesus a happy birthday.

One day we turned the kitchen into a cookie factory. Todd and Niqua rolled and cut dough into Christmas shapes. There was flour everywhere. After the cookies were baked, the kids went to work with bright-colored decorations. What fun we had.

Then we lined boxes with festive Christmas paper and filled them with cookies. We felt like Santa Claus when we delivered the goodies to the hospital and the clinic. We hoped all that we did would reflect the love of Jesus. As the song goes, "Jesus in me loves you."

We were so happy. Todd was doing great! But we felt so sorry for the kids who would be spending Christmas at the hospital.

Once I had seen Rosie Greer at the hospital playing his guitar and entertaining a group of children. That gave us the idea to ask the Pat Boone family to come and sing Christmas carols at the hospital. Dutch got in touch with Mrs. Boone's brother-in-law and Mr. Boone's secretary, both of whom promised to discuss the idea with the family. We didn't expect they would be able to do it, but we thought it worth a try. What a perfect opportunity to witness for Christ!

On Christmas Eve Day, Pat Boone called at our house. His family had just returned from a trip, and several of them had the flu. He had checked with the hospital to ask if they could come and was turned down because of the danger of infection. He was so sorry it didn't work out, and we were too, but we will always remember fondly their willingness to share their Christmas with us.

Todd's blood count was very low again and he developed an infection, so the day after Christmas found us in the hospital. I thought it would be depressing because of the holidays, but it turned out to be one of the fun stays.

Todd had been given a huge inflated Santa for Christmas. Of course, Santa had come along to the hospital. We tied him by the tip of his hat to Todd's IV pole, and he made the rounds with us.

The second bed in Todd's room was empty that night, so we tucked Santa in and pulled the covers up to his chin. Todd giggled at the surprise of the unsuspecting nurse when she found Santa. Then the doctor put on quite a show for Todd, pretending to examine Santa.

Todd loved to pull tricks. One day as he went to the bathroom, I was sitting on the couch right next to the door. Suddenly a swarm of doctors and nurses came running and tore the bathroom door open. I was stunned.

There Todd sat on the "throne," grinning from ear to ear. He had pulled the emergency cord to see what would happen.

One late evening found me roaming the halls, trying to locate my son. The halls were quiet and the playroom was closed, but Todd was nowhere to be found. The head nurse and I looked in all the rooms—no Todd. We discussed calling Security to help in the search.

Then we noticed a flickering light in the dark room across from the nurses' station. We hadn't looked there. It was supposed to be empty.

But there sat Todd, on the lap of a favorite nurse, absorbed in a monster movie on TV.

We were sent home on New Year's Eve. Since Todd had had an infection, he was to continue taking antibiotics. I always made sure that his medicine came in liquid or tablet form, since he simply could not swallow capsules. But in our excitement at being sent home, we didn't realize until late in the evening that we'd been given antibiotics in capsule form. By then it was too late to get another prescription.

Dutch decided Todd would have to learn that night how to swallow capsules. He had me make popcorn, and he broke off small pieces for Todd to swallow. Todd tried over and over again until he was finally able to swallow pieces of popcorn the size of a capsule without water. It hurt just to watch, and I thought it was cruel, but God knew it was necessary for what lay ahead. Todd would put this training to good use.

January brought many trips to the park. My brother Tom was with us for an extended vacation, and he had what a child treasures most: patience and time. He spent many hours with the kids. They explored Verdugo Park, playing on slides and swings, running and pitching and batting. At Griffith Park they rode the merry-go-round and the ponies. Descanso Gardens harbored hungry squirrels that were so tame they came up close to nibble food.

The tram ride through the park gave us an

Dear God

Thank you for our food
I wish you a merry Ch
ristmas and I wish
Jesus a happy Bir
thday. We love you.
Thank you for the
animals. Thank you
for loving us. Than
k you for being

so nice to us. Please
come in our heart.
Please ~~come into~~ bring our
garden Angels. Plea
s get me well. Amen

Todd could really pray. Often we asked him to say the blessing
at the table. Once he decided he would make up a prayer
ahead of time and write it down so he wouldn't have to think
of a new one each time.

exciting overview and helped us get acquainted. There were special paths that only kids could find through the many magnolia trees. And always, Tom had his camera going, following the kids and catching them in natural poses. These pictures are priceless to us, aglow with the quality of the moment they capture.

There was a striking resemblance between Tom and Todd, and they seemed to have a special bond. When Tom left to go back to Canada, Todd was deeply hurt. At the airport he jumped up on Tom, with his arms around Tom's neck, his legs around his waist. I had to tear them apart so Tom could heed the last call for his flight. It was as if Todd knew it was their last good-bye. He cried on the way home.

Since the number and size of Todd's tumors were drastically reduced, the doctors talked about removing a final spot on his lungs surgically, if they could shrink it just a little more and if they found no other evidence of cancer in his body. That meant tests again. Many of them Todd already knew and dreaded.

For one test dye had to be injected into a vein in his foot. Then he had to lie still while a series of X rays were taken. Todd had had this test before, and he knew it would hurt. Again, we tried to prepare him. We explained the procedure and stressed that if he cooperated and lay perfectly still and relaxed as much as possible, it wouldn't hurt as much as if he were tense.

Reluctantly he followed his favorite technician into the X-ray room. Soon I could hear his screams. The noise summoned all available technicians and several doctors.

I was not permitted in the room, so all I could do was sit there and pray. They tried everything to calm him down, but with no success. After some time, I was called in.

Todd was in hysterics. He fought like a lion. There was no way to get close to him to inject the dye into his bloodstream. My presence didn't help at all. There was nothing I could do. Soon I was close to hysterics, too. I thought they would have to have several men hold him down, but the doctor decided against that and called the test off. They took some X rays without the dye.

Todd and I were emotionally and physically exhausted. The X-ray technician was crying. She vowed never again to become personally involved with a patient. She couldn't bear to see Todd so upset.

I found myself hoping the tests would show that Todd's cancer had spread, because I didn't want the doctors to operate on his lungs. I despaired of the thought of them cutting away at him again. I had it all figured out. God would miraculously heal Todd, and everyone would have to bow to the evidence of God's love and intervention in our lives. He would not have to share the credit with the doctors.

But Dutch vowed never to give up. As long as there was *anything* the doctors could use, he wanted them to try, even if it was experimental.

Our next visit to the clinic was supposed to be routine. We weren't prepared for the doctor's words: "The drugs have lost their effectiveness. The tumors are growing again."

The meaning of his words sank in slowly. Deliberately I tried to think, "Praise God from whom all blessings flow." But the thought was painful. The praise was not spontaneous. And yet, in a way, I was relieved. There would be no more surgery, at least for now. I was sure this was just a temporary setback.

January 19 saw us back at Shrine Auditorium for a miracle service. Our hopes soared as we asked God to touch and heal Todd. We praised God for the healings we witnessed, and the music of the powerful choir lifted our hearts.

It was hard for Todd to sit. He asked if he could lie down somewhere. There was a couch in the restroom, but I was reluctant to take him there. Healing was taking place in the auditorium. Would we miss ours if we left?

Then I realized the Holy Spirit would find us anywhere. "Here I am with my child, Father.

You know we are here. Help us not to be discouraged."

But on the way home, it was hard not to be disappointed. Still, we knew Jesus was in control and we trusted him to know what was best for us.

11

The Lord had once again been sending me the Lord's Prayer. I tried to prepare myself, knowing from experience what would come. I had come to think that the blessed words of the Lord's Prayer were prophesies of doom to me. Then, with unending love and patience, the Holy Spirit showed me that if he warned me with the Lord's Prayer, that meant he already knew what was going to happen. Whatever the future held was part of God's plan. He was in control, and he would see us through.

Todd asked me once, "Mom, why am I sick? Why might I have to die?"

(*Oh, dear God, please give me words to say.*)

One of Todd's favorite TV shows involved a maze. There were two players, usually a husband-and-wife team. He would stand on a platform, overlooking a seven-foot-maze. She would race against time to get through the maze to a designated point. If she did not obey his commands immediately, she would lose her direction and precious time.

With this example I explained to Todd (and myself) that God is on a platform, overlooking our lives. He knows what is best for us and how best to fulfill his plan for us. Only as we follow his direction do we arrive at the right point. We trust God to know what is best for us.

Todd never questioned God's will again. But there were many questions in my heart. Todd had weathered so many storms, he was prepared for anything. But if he was going to die, what was the preparation for?

Should we continue to ask for healing for Todd, or were we just being selfish? Maybe he had suffered enough. Maybe his mission here had come to an end. Even if the Lord healed him of cancer, he would probably suffer some other kind of illness or injury during his lifetime. I couldn't bear to see him hurt any more. Everybody had to die sometime. Even Lazarus died again eventually. Perhaps now was as good a time as any for Todd.

One late evening I desperately needed to pour out my heart to someone—to pray, to talk, to find fresh insight. I called my friend Dona and she invited me to her house to talk. This is how she remembers that night:

Todd was low again and it was constant care for him, as he always felt the need of you close by. Niqua, too, was pulling on you, and I know you were at your wit's end. You were tired and the doctor had said the tumors were growing, so you felt sad.

We talked about Todd's life and how through his illness you had grown to depend on Jesus. You asked if you should pray for an extended life for Todd, and I shared with you the story of Hezekiah (2 Kings 20 and 2 Chron. 32:20-33). Hezekiah prayed to be healed. God answered and gave him an additional 15 years. He had been a good king, but he became proud and showed those who came from Babylon his riches. It was all taken from him and carried to Babylon. Even his sons became a part of wicked Babylon. His son Manasseh, born during the 15 years, was the worst king of Judah.

The Lord knew our hearts. If taking Todd would glorify him more and reveal a deep love for him in you and Dutch, then I knew that was his perfect will. We talked of his faithfulness and how his strength is made perfect in weakness and how he wants wholeness either way, for life here or in heaven. Todd would be whole. He could extend Todd's life, but would that be best? Would the miracle glorify him more, or would your walk during these days of suffering glorify him more?

Finally, when I didn't know how to pray or what to pray for anymore, God showed me Romans 8:26-27:

Likewise the Spirit helps us in our weakness; for we do not know how to pray as we ought, but the Spirit himself intercedes for us with sighs too deep for words. And he who searches the hearts of men knows what is the mind of the Spirit, because the Spirit intercedes for the saints according to the will of God.

And Philippians 4:6-7:

Have no anxiety about anything, but in everything by prayer and supplication with thanksgiving let your requests be made known to God. And the peace of God, which passes all understanding, will keep your hearts and your minds in Christ Jesus.

I usually looked forward to the evening hours when the children would be in bed and I'd have a chance to relax and gather my thoughts

112

in prayer. But late in Todd's illness my mother made me aware of my selfishness: "All day long Todd is busy, playing and talking, but at night, in those moments before going to sleep, he is left alone to dwell on his illness and entertain thoughts about death. You ought to stay with him and read to him."

Todd did have frequent nightmares. I told him to call on Jesus for help, even in his dreams. I wanted him to lean on Jesus for all his needs. Several days later he told me with beaming face, "Mom! It worked! I had a bad dream and I asked Jesus to help, and he did!"

When Todd and I had special times together, when he knew how much I loved him, I told him that Jesus loved him much more than I. How was he to understand the Lord's love except as an infinite multiplication of the love we showed him?

Todd's early fears that shots were meant to kill him taught us that there were many opportunities for misunderstandings, many opportunities for fear to creep in. Countless times I would ask him, "Son, are you wondering about anything?" to give him an opportunity to talk things over.

At times, just seeing the expression on people's faces when they learned that he had *cancer* caused him to wonder anew if we were hiding anything from him. He saw their pity and concern and it triggered self-pity in him. We had a talk about that also.

"Todd, don't let it bother you when people roll their eyes and get that funny look on their face when they hear you have cancer. They just know that means surgery and lots of X rays and shots and IVs, and that you have a lot of pain. But you've already had all of that, and you know what it's like, so it doesn't have to scare you anymore. The worst that can happen to you now is that you die and go to heaven. But that would be OK. Then you would be with Jesus."

On one of Todd's last days in school I was left without a car to pick him up. No problem —he had walked many times. But at the last moment it started to rain. What could I do? Sometimes in the past one of the other mothers had given him a ride home, so I hoped she would see him walking today and offer him a lift. I prayed while he was on his way home.

He arrived dripping wet. "How come you didn't get me?"

"I'm sorry, but I didn't have a car. I've been praying for Jesus to get you home safely."

"Well, OK. At least you tried."

Honesty and openness were of major importance. Todd needed to be able to trust us. We were a buffer between him and the things causing pain. We would be informed by the

114

staff of upcoming tests and try to prepare him. If we didn't know what was to be done, we told him that. When we had to take sides against him and help hold him down, he knew we had no other choice.

Once Todd's emotions boiled over. He thought I had lied to him. I had promised that the IV now in his vein would not have to be restarted. When the medicine was all in his bloodstream and the bottle of IV fluid was empty, there would be no more IV this time around. I failed to caution, though, that this only held true if the IV did not infiltrate.

When a vein becomes brittle it may leak, or the needle may touch the wall of the vein or even penetrate it. Then fluid leaks into the tissue rather than into the bloodstream, causing swelling.

On her rounds that day the head nurse checked Todd's hand. It was swollen. The IV was infiltrated. With swift moves, she removed the tape holding the needle in place and pulled the IV out.

Todd was furious. I had promised no more IV. Now it would have to be restarted.

He went into a tantrum. He picked up and threw everything in the room—his toys, the medication tray, the blood pressure gauge, a lamp, books, the radio. He was wild. It was as if he had blown a fuse, and all of his frustration was coming to the surface.

I couldn't stop him. Tears came to my eyes, and I knew I had to get out. I called Dutch. "You've got to come right now. Todd's gone crazy. He won't listen to me. I can't handle it. I'm not going back in there until you come."

The head nurse walked out of the room shortly after me. She thought Todd would calm down best when left alone.

Some time later I could hear Todd in the hall. I didn't join him. I was hurt, humiliated, and angry. How could he create a scene like that!

I determined that Todd would pick up every last thing he'd thrown by himself, but Dutch had better insight than I. When he arrived I expected him to scold Todd severely. Instead, he calmly started picking up some things in Todd's room. "Come, Son, let me help you pick this up." His quiet support broke the ice of resistance, and soon we were discussing what had happened.

We explained that, while we could not condone his action, we did understand the frustration and disappointment that lead to it. Todd felt that I betrayed him. Just a simple misunderstanding, but of what consequence!

Many marriages suffer under the test of the stress of a major illness in the family. When people are hurting, reason is clouded and tempers flare. They disagree over actions to be taken, treatments to be sought or omitted. To others they are polite and courteous—one must save face, create an illusion of being on top of the situation. But in front of the mate all barriers drop. The easiest one to lash out at, to hurl all your anger at, is the one closest to you.

But for the most part God spared us. As we leaned on the Lord, we could lean on each other for help, encouragement, and support. Whenever I had all I could take and thought all hope was lost, Dutch took over. When he couldn't stand to be at the hospital, I was there. We could laugh together and cry together. Rather than driving us apart, this seeming tragedy in our lives bonded us closer together.

I was more concerned about the effect on Niqua. She was often pushed around and left behind. Todd clung to me and demanded more and more of my time, so Niqua had to play second fiddle. My mother cared for her as well if not better than I, but Niqua had to cope with a lot of stress and tension.

Then the Lord began to show Niqua to me in a new light. Eventually I came to see the quiet strength of my four-year-old. The Lord would strengthen her in her own time, and he would guide her through the life he had planned for her.

12

One day as I sat in the hall, two mothers got on the elevator. One was crying. I had heard that her daughter was near death. I so much wanted to console her and tell her about Jesus, but I was too timid to approach her. I prayed that God would have her walk up to me upon her return and start a conversation, if I was to witness to her.

While I was waiting, I opened my Bible at random and read:

> Truly, truly, I say to you, unless a grain of wheat falls into the earth and dies, it remains alone; but if it dies, it bears much fruit. He who loves his life loses it, and he who hates his life in this world will keep it for eternal life. If any one serves me, he

119

> must follow me; and where I am, there
> shall my servant be also; if anyone serves
> me, the Father will honor him (John 12:
> 24-26).

I turned the page and read on:

> Let not your hearts be troubled; believe
> in God, believe also in me. In my Father's
> house are many rooms; if it were not so,
> would I have told you that I go to prepare
> a place for you? And when I go and pre-
> pare a place for you, I will come again and
> will take you to myself, that where I am
> you may be also (John 14:1-6).

Was the Lord speaking to me through his
Word, preparing me for Todd's death? Was he
saying that this grain of wheat would fall into
the ground, too, and bear much fruit?

I never did talk to that other mother. I had
so much to ponder myself.

The doctors had one more drug they could
try. It was experimental. They were not sure
of the dosage or of all the side effects or of its
effectiveness. But it was potent. Unlike most
IV fluids, it burned as it entered the vein.

A doctor came each day as the drug was administered to observe Todd's reactions. She
would ask Todd about any tingling sensation,
pain, or discomfort he was feeling. Since the
drug was administered through an IV over a

120

period of several hours, to pass the time she invented all sorts of games to play with Todd while she observed him. Once she promised to bring her makeup the next day and transform Todd into a roaring tiger. He could hardly wait. He didn't mind answering her questions from then on.

The next day he lay perfectly still as she transformed him into a ferocious animal. The only thing that moved was Todd's mouth, which couldn't help but break into a wide grin once in a while. Finally he found the words to express his total joy: "This is even more funner than Disneyland!"

For the next day Denise promised to bring a tail, some whiskers, and clothing to complete the costume. But by that time the chemotherapy had shown its side effects. Todd was feeling so poorly that he was no longer interested. There was no way to duplicate the bliss he had felt the day before.

When people came to visit, they often felt awkward. What could they say? We usually made small talk. "How are you?" "Hanging in there. . . . Holding up." Sometimes their words came across like a pat on a child's head and a "There, there, it's going to be all right." Often well-meaning people would say: "I understand what you're going through."

I felt like screaming sometimes. I wanted to

take people by the shoulders and shake them. How could they understand? Had they ever been one of five people to hold down a little child so an injection could be given? Had they ever stood helplessly by and listened to a child's screams of pain and frustration, trying to find soothing words to calm him when they felt like screaming themselves?

Even if they did understand, I didn't acknowledge it. But I knew Jesus was there, and he understood. He knew what pain was like. He knew what it meant to suffer. I could be honest with him. "O God, I hurt! I can't stand it anymore. Please help us!" He was there to comfort—to give the peace that passes all understanding. He allowed tears to flow and dried them when relief came.

The tumors were growing; the pressure grew. I had been at the hospital with Todd several days without going home. My physical needs were taken care of. I was permitted to use a shower on the floor, and Dutch or my mother supplied me with fresh clothing.

But one night I'd had all I could take emotionally. Todd was in pain and wanted me at his side constantly. I'd had to calm him down, encourage him, and care for him until I had no more to give. Once more I placed a desperate phone call home. "Please, honey, you have to come, so I can get out. I've got to get away!"

Even though Dutch had to go to work the next day, he came to sit with Todd during the night. But Todd did not want me to leave. He was used to having me anticipate his needs before he asked.

"Please! Mom, stay! Don't leave me! I'll do *anything* you want me to do. But please don't leave."

"Dad is here with you," I offered. "You won't be alone. He will take good care of you."

"Yes, I know, but I want you here," he insisted.

"Son, I'm all confused and upset. I have to go home and talk to Jesus for a while and ask him to help us."

"But you can talk to him here!"

"Yes, but I have to get away for a while. I'll be back in the morning," I promised.

I fled the room, the fourth floor, the hospital, and managed to hold back the flood of tears until I reached the car and was headed for home.

About halfway home, I noticed the car radio was playing, "Turn your eyes upon Jesus." That was the answer! I had taken my eyes off Jesus and looked to all our trouble. I opened my Bible to the front flyleaf and wrote, "Keep your eyes upon Jesus." At home I fell into bed and slept without interruption until morning.

The next evening I was pushing Todd around

the halls. He loved to go around and around. Once he invented a new game. Equipped with some scraps of paper and a pencil, he handed out tickets to nurses for speeding as they hurried past us on their rounds.

But tonight Todd wasn't feeling well. He was quiet as we walked. Then I glanced at his hand. I had learned to watch that IV like a hawk. I thought I noticed swelling. The IV was going bad.

I stopped to take a closer look, and Todd panicked. "*No!* I don't want you to look at it. You'll just tell the nurse it's infiltrated and she'll pull it and then they'll start another one."

A thought flashed through my mind. The only reason the IV was needed was to keep the vein open for the last dose of chemotherapy the next day. This last round of chemotherapy had shown no results at all. What if tomorrow's chemotherapy weren't given?

"Son," I said, "I'll tell you what. You go back to your room and wait there for me while I go call Dad. I want to ask him if the IV has to be restarted if it's infiltrated. I can't promise you anything, but I'll ask."

I called home, but Dutch wasn't there yet. I left word everywhere I could think of for him to call me as soon as possible.

In the hall I met two doctors familiar with Todd's case. One had taken care of Todd all along. We valued his judgment. Todd loved him. He cared.

"Doctor," I began, "I think Todd's IV is infiltrated, but he is so scared of having to have it restarted that he won't let me check it. Dutch and I have already decided that if this series of chemotherapy shows no results, we're going to quit—no more experiments. My question is this: Will it make any difference in the long run if he has that last dose tomorrow?"

The doctors looked at each other, their eyes pleading for an answer from the other one. "Oh, Mrs. Monson! Don't put us on the spot like this! We can't make that decision for you."

"But I just want you to tell me if you think this last dose will make a difference. I don't think so. But I never want to have to look back and say, 'If only. . . .' "

"Well, truthfully, the therapy has not had any significant effect. Who is to say what one more dose would do? You and your husband have to decide. But I really don't think that it will make any difference. If it was going to have an impact, we would have seen it by now."

"Thank you, doctor, that's all I wanted to know. I'll talk to my husband tonight about stopping the therapy."

I didn't offer any more hope to Todd. We had to wait for Dutch's call. I kept my promise to leave the IV alone until a decision had been made.

"Mrs. Monson, there's a call for you at the desk," the nurse said. Normally such calls were discouraged. They tied up needed lines. But the whole staff seemed to know that we were about to make a major decision. The intern hovered nearby, trying not to show that he was listening. Our doctor had already told him to abide by our decision.

"Honey," I explained, "Todd's IV looks like it might be infiltrated, and he's so scared about having it restarted. I talked to the doctor and he's not sure one more dose would make that much difference."

Dutch was calm when he replied, "Well, there's only so much you can do. If it isn't going to make much difference, it's more important that Todd isn't hurt any more than has to be. Go ahead and tell them to stop if the IV infiltrates. If it doesn't, we'll go ahead with the dose. If it does, we'll leave it at that."

A few months earlier Dutch had vowed to try anything and everything medical science had to offer. He'd said we would fight to the end. Now God had given him the strength to place quality of life above quantity and trust the Lord for the outcome.

The intern came right over after I hung up. He had heard. His concern was apparent. I told him I would tell Todd of our decision and then they could check the IV.

"Son, we've decided that it's up to Jesus alone to heal you now. There will be no more chemotherapy, no more IVs, no more tests, no more shots, except for pain. But Dad said we should give it a chance. If the IV doesn't infiltrate, you'll get the chemotherapy tomorrow, and then that will be it. If it does infiltrate, we'll pull it and that's the end of IVs. It won't be restarted."

His face brightened, "You mean it? No more? What if the doctors talk to you and change your mind?"

"I've already talked to them about it. No more IV after this. Promise."

He was so happy, so relieved. I don't know that he understood the full significance of our decision, but he was grateful. At the moment the status of the IV was "marginal." Later it proved to be infiltrated, and it was pulled. For days after that Todd's hand was sore and blue from the fluid that had leaked into the tissue.

There were no more treatments to try. We wanted to go home. Todd wanted to go home. While he was at the hospital he was never quite sure that we wouldn't change our mind about the IV. At home he was safe.

Then it was time to pack. As usual the room was full of our personal belongings—pillows and blankets from home to be more comfortable, a lamp so I could read at night, pictures of Jesus, toys and teddy bears, games, and projects.

While Dutch settled with the cashier, I received last minute instructions from the doctor. He prescribed cough medicine with codeine, but he didn't expect it to do much good. Todd's tumors were obstructing his lungs, and the body's natural reflex was to expel the obstruction by coughing. Todd had been chewing on ice when he felt the urge to cough. Whether it really helped or not didn't matter. He thought it helped. It curbed his anxiety.

There was Tylenol with codeine for the pain and Thorazine to tranquilize him. The quieter he remained, the less he would fight to breathe, and the easier it would be for him. We were to start with small doses and increase them as his pain and his tolerance for the drugs grew.

Todd's blood count was low. Under normal circumstances he would have been given a blood transfusion, but the low count had the advantage of making him drowsy, so he was less aware of pain. The transfusion might perk him up for a couple days, but would make it harder in the long run. We decided against it.

His lung X rays showed shadows that could be interpreted as water. To relieve pressure in his chest, the doctors could try to tap the water with a long needle inserted between the ribs, but it would be unpleasant and the water would quickly return. We decided against it.

We were grateful that the doctors were frank and did not recommend unnecessary treatments.

We made an appointment for Todd to be seen in clinic about a week later.

"How long do we have, doctor?"

"About two weeks."

We found a toy wagon and piled all our belongings onto it, with Todd on top. Our departure resembled a circus parade. Todd's triumphant exit. All the nurses lined up to say good-bye.

"Look at the king on his throne!"

"Take care!"

"See you."

"Thank you."

"Bye! I'm going home!"

13

Most of us live as if we're going to exist forever here on this earth. We seldom think about our days being numbered.

What do you do when you are told you have two weeks left? Two weeks to cram all your feelings into; two weeks in which to do all the things you've always wanted to do, to say all the things you wanted to be sure to say; two weeks in which to live a whole lifetime.

One night in the car on the way home from the grocery store I heard Evie sing, "If Jesus comes tomorrow, we've got just one more day." Thoughts started whirling in my mind. I left the groceries to be unpacked later and tried to put those thoughts down on paper.

The next day I asked Dutch to give my

"poem" to Pastor Roufs to see what he thought of it. This is how he had it printed in the next church newsletter:

> There is a song that goes: "If Jesus comes tomorrow, we've got just one more day!"
>
> A week ago they said Todd had two weeks left. But whether Jesus comes, or we go, we've all got just one more day because we have no guarantee for even a minute.
>
> How different would we live ("Take up your cross and follow me"), love, and forgive, if we kept in mind that if Jesus comes tomorrow, then we've got just one more day!
>
> There are so many yet to be told of our Lord's love and gift of salvation, so many to be helped, led to the well that never will run dry—people contacted, smiles given, priorities felt, lessons learned and shared.
>
> But if Jesus comes tomorrow, we've got just one more day. Jesus said, "Would that you were cold or hot! So, because you are lukewarm, and neither cold nor hot, I will spew you out of my mouth" (Rev. 3:15-16).
>
> Did we do all we could, or are there things left to be done?
>
> Because: If Jesus comes tomorrow, then we've got just one more day!

How many more times would we tell our kids, husbands, wives, or parents, "I love you—I'm thankful God gave you to me," if we knew we had just one more day?

Our stomachs are full and we plan progressive dinners while charitable organizations need food to give to the starving.

If Jesus comes tomorrow. . . .

We forget that Jesus died for us. We forget that God stood by and did nothing while Jesus paid for our sins. We forget there are so many people who don't know about their gift of life.

If Jesus comes tomorrow!

We busy ourselves with life and drown out our feelings and the voice that said: "Behold! I stand at the door and knock."

Yet, if Jesus comes tomorrow, then we've got just one more day!

There was to be a short play performed by children at one of the schools. Some of Todd's friends were in the play, so we were invited to come to the performance. I didn't know if Todd would be up to it, but he promised to rest beforehand so he would be strong enough to go.

We packed several thermos bottles full of ice, his constant companion now. He would chew it by the handful whenever he felt the urge to cough. He sat on my lap and enjoyed the performance.

Afterward we had to go up an incline to get to the car. Once Todd would have run up that driveway. Now he had to take it very slowly, one step at a time. He was so weak, and the air capacity in his lungs was so small. I couldn't carry him—he thought that hurt more than walking. I could only support him slightly.

Finally we made it to the car. I planned to take Todd home.

"No, Mom, let's go to Verdugo Park for a while. *Please!* I'll even talk to you. About Jesus or anything. Just let's go."

It was one of those rare days with bright sunshine and clear blue skies. We found a nice spot in Todd's favorite park and sat cherishing God's beautiful world. He leaned against me, chewing his ice, for an hour.

A man was throwing a ball for his little puppy. Time and time again the dog would run after it so fast that he tripped over his own little legs and rolled in the grass. Todd giggled and longed for his dog King. He hoped King was waiting for him in heaven.

Reluctantly, we left, but we didn't return home. We stopped by Todd's school. School was out, but the teachers were still there.

Todd came to say good-bye. I knew it; Todd

knew it; the teachers knew it. Yet none of us said so.

Todd hadn't been to school for a while so he was eager to say hi to all the mice, hampsters, and other animals the class took care of. It was a private moment as he sat on the floor in front of the little cages. A warm embrace from his teacher, which he endured in spite of the pain, marked the end of our little visit.

A sad little boy sat down in the car. Then his first grade teacher came running out, trying to hide her tears. By then Todd was so tired physically and emotionally that he hardly responded.

The principal was not there, but he came to the house later. Todd was proud that his principal would come and practice cursive writing with him. His visit meant very much to Todd.

His teacher came a number of times, bringing piles of cards the children had made for Todd. They were decorated with all kinds of things. Some even popped out when opened. It had been our practice to display all cards along the walls in his room, but there were so many now that we ran out of room.

Then his teacher had the class write compositions, and she brought them by so Todd could correct and grade them. He worked hard, trying to be fair and kind in grading them. What an honor it was for him! We encouraged him to take his time, but he wanted to get them done. And perhaps he knew best. Had he waited, he probably would not have had the strength to finish them.

All through his illness, we had tried to talk to Todd about what was going to happen to him so he would be prepared. We thought that would take away some of the fear of the unknown. But this was different. We thought he was going to die. How could we tell him that?

Once he said, "I must be getting better, or you would be taking me to a miracle service." We didn't have the heart to crush that flicker of hope. Always in the past when things were rough, we would promise that little by little, each day, he would feel better. How could we prepare him for feeling worse each day?

So we said nothing.

But he knew when he said his good-byes.

He knew when we had our last hour in the park.

He knew when he got out a piece of paper and wrote:

Jesus I Double Love you

14

Where should we put Todd's bed? Where would he be most comfortable? Where would he die?

The bedrooms were private, but they were down a narrow hall. The living room was large and we could put a bed in the middle, but it didn't have a door for privacy and it was too close to the kitchen. Still, it was close to the *front* door.

The thing that loomed so large in my mind was: How would we get his little body out of the house after. . . . The living room was closest to the front door, so I could disappear into one of the bedrooms while they took him. I asked a cousin who had lost a child how she could bear to watch them take the body from the house. The more I thought about it, the bigger the problem seemed.

Dutch settled the matter. Todd would be in his own bedroom, surrounded by his favorite things, away from the noise of the telephone and the kitchen. Of course.

Then it was time for our appointment in clinic. Todd had not been out of the house for several days. When Dutch carried him to the car, he started to scream. We couldn't understand why.

"We're just going for a talk with the doctor. What are you screaming about?"

He was so busy trying to catch his breath that he couldn't answer. We shook our heads.

X rays confirmed our suspicions that Todd was much worse. We tried to talk to the doctor without Todd. We suggested to Todd that he propel himself around in a wheelchair for a while. He kept bumping his wheelchair into our door, hoping it would "accidentally" open so he could hear what we were discussing. He was still afraid we would plot further treatments and hospitalization. Dutch went out to be with him and kept him occupied while I continued to talk with the doctor. He had no new suggestions.

On our way out I mentioned to the nurse how difficult it was to get Todd to swallow codeine pills. We felt that he was in more pain than need be simply because he was so reluctant to take those tablets. "If only they came in capsule form," I sighed. "He could swallow capsules."

She looked astonished. "Don't you know that you can buy empty gelatin capsules? All you have to do is crush the tablets between two spoons and then put the powder into the capsules."

We got the capsules and Todd was able to swallow them without much trouble, even after he could swallow no more water. Now he could be relatively pain-free.

Dutch went ahead to drive the car right up to the front of the hospital. As we got close to the automatic doors, Todd panicked again and screamed, "Don't go out those doors!"

"Why? Do you want to stay here?"

"No! But don't go out those doors."

"Son, how are you going to get home if we don't go out those doors?"

He was red in the face, gasping for air and hurting. Dutch turned off the engine and came in to see what was holding us up. He figured out that the fresh air and slight breeze were too much for Todd's diseased lungs to handle. "Hold both your hands over your mouth and nose, son, and I'll carry you out to the car real quick. We'll keep the windows closed. Maybe that will help."

We got home without further delay.

Grandpa and Grandma Monson came to stay with us. My first selfish reaction was, "I don't need company on top of everything else." But they weren't company. They took charge of the kitchen. They cleaned house. They answered the telephone. They were there to offer strength and support.

Grandma had lost her brother several months earlier to cancer. She knew the pain of loss. She was resigned to losing Todd and hoped for all our sakes that it would be over soon.

But her resignation spurred me on. No! I was not ready for Todd to go! I cherished every moment. I wouldn't let him go until I absolutely had to. Besides, who said he was going anyway? It wasn't too late for the Lord to intervene in a miraculous way.

My mother and sister took care of Niqua. She spent most of her nights at their apartment a few blocks away. During the day she was home, playing with Todd until he grew less and less tolerant of her. We didn't realize how much she was emotionally affected until we found her several times hiding in corners or behind furniture crying.

It was time for her to leave. She couldn't be around Todd any longer. She went to stay with friends.

Niqua was to see Todd just one more time.

Her Sunday school teacher gave her a picture of Jesus to give to Todd. Timidly, Niqua came into the room to give him the picture. He greeted her with a smile (rare by then). He was really happy about the picture. He asked me to hang it where he could see it.

Dutch and I were with Todd constantly now. We took turns sleeping in Niqua's bed, or one of us would sneak out into the adjoining bedroom for a few hours of sleep.

It was easiest for Todd to breathe sitting straight up. Many times I sat behind him in bed to support him, but then that became too uncomfortable for him. We gathered most of our pillows and were always busy rearranging them to keep him as comfortable as possible. They were piled high on either side of him to lift his arms and extend them out from his chest so they would not place additional pressure on his lungs.

He was so thin. Often I forced back tears when I felt his shoulder, which was nothing but a small ball of bone by now. His rectum protruded; there was no flesh to hide it.

Mother borrowed a portable TV set from a friend so Todd could watch from his bed. There was a record player to play his favorite records. I thought I would scream if I had to listen to "Little Toot" one more time. At 2:00 in the morning or 3:00 in the afternoon (he never slept, only dozed off and on): "Please, Mom, play 'Little Toot.'"

The radio was always playing softly, tuned to a local Christian station. It was barely audible, but an air of worship and praise filled the room.

We played endless games. His mind was still sharp. He loved to beat us at Monopoly, and he won most of the hangman games. He painstakingly colored a picture of Easter Bunny surrounded by flowers and Easter eggs, to be submitted in a coloring contest.

Mother and I took turns massaging his legs. At the hospital, we had turned the massage into a guessing game. I would write words or designs on his back with lotion, and he tried to "read" them by feeling. Now he just wanted his arms and legs massaged.

We didn't want him to get bedsores on his heels. He liked it best when we rubbed and pressed the bottom of his feet. Often I would curl up by his feet while I massaged them. If he dozed off, I would close my eyes for a few minutes of rest, only to have him awaken with a start and cry, "Push, Mom, push!" And, again, I pressed on the soles of his feet.

I developed the habit of rocking myself back and forth constantly in an effort to stay awake. Somehow it seemed to help my nerves, too. I retained that habit until much later when Dutch called my attention to it.

Once as I sat behind Todd to support him, we were looking out his bedroom window. The day was windy and heavy storm clouds hung in the sky. I commented on how the birds had to struggle and fight to fly in such a wind. Todd thought for a while before he said, "I don't think they're fighting. I think they're just sailing along with the wind."

That truth applied to his illness. Todd wasn't fighting the storm in his life. He, too, was sailing along with the wind.

We called Todd's brother John in Iowa and told him that it was time for him to come if he wanted to see Todd again. I did so with reservation. Wouldn't John's arrival and all the extra attention demonstrate to Todd how little hope we held for his recovery? We still had not told him that he was dying. Yes, he knew, but we had not been able to talk about it. When we told Todd that John was coming, he smiled. He was glad. My fears were unfounded.

Todd was very sensitive to smell by now. If we had brushed our teeth or washed our hands with soap, he would shout, "Get away from me! You smell!" We couldn't eat in his room; it smelled too much. There was no food we could tempt him with. One of his last cravings was

143

for pizza, but when we got one from his favorite pizza place, he never ate it.

We had to refuse visitors. They caused too much excitement. And they, too, "smelled." We couldn't open the window any further, or close it either. If he thought I was adjusting the heat vent, he screamed. Any change in the air current frightened him.

His breathing had become so loud and labored, it could be heard halfway through the house. Each breath could be his last. Which one would it be?

"O God, stop his suffering, but not with this breath. Just one more, please, just one more."

He did usually let Pastor Roufs in when he came because he knew he would pray for him. Pastor disconnected the doorbell for us when that, too, became disturbing.

People found many ways to let us know they cared and were praying. They lent us equipment to help us keep Todd supplied with ice. Flowers from a wedding appeared at our doorstep. "We know you couldn't be with us, so we wanted to share with you." My mother was forever thinking of new ways to keep Todd more comfortable—a sheepskin to make his bed softer, a roll for his head, a bedpan with a thick rubber cushion. Since he was just skin and bones, sitting on a plain bedpan would have been painful.

A note touched my heart:

> My thoughts are with you. God will bear you up as long as you need it. Perhaps you have wanted to take Todd's place; perhaps you would like to carry him through this valley yourself. God knows best. God knows you.

And there was Scripture:

> O the depth of the riches and wisdom and knowledge of God! How unsearchable are his judgments and how inscrutable his ways (Rom. 11:33).

> Eye hath not seen, nor ear heard, neither have entered into the heart of man, the things which God hath prepared for them that love him (1 Cor. 2:9 KJV).

The companionship and openness of a mother whose daughter had died of leukemia a few months earlier were invaluable to me. I could ask her questions I could ask no one else. And she was willing to share. She was also living proof to me that life goes on after a child dies.

Three elders from Church on the Way came to pray.

"Son, there are three men here who want to pray for you. I can't promise that they won't smell. Can they come in?"

They prayed over him, laid hands on him,

145

and anointed him again with oil. They came from the room weeping for Todd.

Our doctor left word at the hospital switchboard to pass our calls through to him at home. Several times I called during the night in desperation, "Are you sure there is nothing else we can do?"

Then came a letter addressed to Todd. The stationery had a picture of a frog on it. Todd asked me to read it for him. When I was halfway through, I realized the writer assumed that Todd knew he was on his way to heaven. I wanted to stop! But there was no way out. I had to finish reading it:

Dear Todd,

Frogs always look as though they are smiling, and I guess that is why I like this paper. God has made so many interesting animals and also many beautiful places for them to live. When I know that heaven is so much more wonderful than our earth, I can hardly imagine the beautiful places to see.

My husband went to live with Jesus awhile ago, Todd, and I sometimes imagine how happy he must be there. It is where he wanted to be and I know Jesus took him there by the hand so he was not afraid to leave us. When I go to heaven, I know so many of my friends will be there that I sometimes think it will be like a big party. When you go to heaven you will get to see Jesus face to face and he will hold you in his arms. Remember we care for you.

I could see Todd's relief. This loving note answered his questions. Our friend had faced the issue squarely when we were still reluctant to do so.

I knew time was running out. If God didn't act soon. . . .

"O God! Is he really going to die? Are you really going to take him? I was hoping for a last-minute miracle, Lord. If you are really going to take him, send me the Lord's Prayer again so I know. But I won't accept it as being a message from you if I read it in my Bible or hear it on Christian radio. That could be coincidence. You'll have to find some other way."

One hour later, the mailman came with a letter from Nancy. She had simply copied the Lord's Prayer word for word.

15

"Ice!" He was constantly chewing chips of ice. He had grown to depend on them and was afraid to be without. He could no longer drink anything, so the ice provided much-needed moisture, but his tongue was becoming raw. We offered M & Ms as a substitute, and he did eat some, but he still did not want to be without his ice. As soon as the bowl was halfway empty, he asked us to refill it. If he dozed off for a few minutes, he woke up screaming, "Ice!"

The popcorn training was now paying off. He was able to swallow capsules without water when he could swallow nothing else.

"Mom, let me walk out into the living room and sit for a while."

"I can't promise that it won't smell out there."

"That's OK. Just bring my M & Ms."

"Where can I hold you so it doesn't hurt you?"

"I'm not hurting."

It took all his strength to wobble out and sit on the couch in the living room, but soon he was uncomfortable and tired and he wanted back in his bed.

"Mom, wheel me around." At the hospital I would get a wheelchair and we would walk the halls by the hour, but here there was no wheelchair. So I threw a rug upside down on the hardwood floor of his room and set the rocking chair on it. Supported by pillows on all sides, he tried to get comfortable while I pushed him back and forth. But it wasn't like riding in a wheelchair, and soon he was tired of it.

"Ice!"

In the hospital he was used to having me around to wait on his every need, but now, as he grew weaker, he preferred to have his dad close to him, to hold his hand.

Many times Dutch and Todd exchanged little affirmations of their love for each other.

"Loves you, Son."

"Loves you, Dad."

Dutch and I would take turns sleeping in the other room—if Todd would let Dutch get away. Many times Dutch slept in Niqua's bed, pushed up close to Todd's holding his hand as he slept. Dutch was so exhausted that it never took long before he started snoring. Then Todd would tickle him and say, "Stop that!" Finally he requested his pen with the long feather on the end of it, and every time Dutch snored, Todd would reach over with his feather and tickle his dad to get him to quit snoring.

Todd's breathing could easily be heard in the other bedroom where we went to sleep. Each time I took a nap I hoped that I wouldn't hear that breathing when I woke up—yet at the same time I frantically prayed I would.

As we hovered over Todd day after day, we would have done anything to relieve his suffering. But we were helpless. There was nothing we could do. I thought I now understood what it must have been like for God the Father during the crucifixion. He stood by and did nothing while Jesus, the Son, was crucified for our sin.

Every time Todd exhaled, I waited anxiously for him to inhale again. Once, in desperation, I wished I could put a pillow over his face and end it all. I felt guilty for a long time for even thinking such a thing. Dutch later admitted he'd had similar thoughts. But the Lord knows our hearts, and he has forgiven us.

Finally I admitted to Dutch that I was frightened of being alone in the room when death came. He announced that I was not to be left alone under any circumstances. Someone was to sit with me so I would not be so scared.

Grandpa came and sat quietly. I was glad he didn't talk. He was just there lending his support. My fear lessened.

Pastor Roufs called to say he and Mrs. Roufs would be out of town for a day, but he wanted us to know where they could be reached.

"Do you think it will be much longer?" he asked.

"I don't see how he can get much worse and still be alive," I replied.

"Don't be ashamed of your tears. When death comes, you will cry. That's normal. I want you to know that," he explained.

"I feel fine. I won't cry."

"You'll see. When death comes, there will be tears."

Monday night we were all gathered around Todd's bed to watch Billy Graham on TV. His sermon topic was angels. He spoke of how angels would come to pick us up and take us to heaven when our time came.

Then Dutch read to Todd from Todd's Bible story book and talked with him about the story.

"Son, I have to ask you one more time, just to be sure: Did you ask Jesus to come into your heart?"

"Oh, Dad, you know I did. I love Jesus."

By midnight Todd had quieted down considerably. His breathing was much shallower and slower. He was dozing frequently. We had increased his dose of medication to two capsules every half hour, but suddenly he did not seem to need them anymore.

I still had not told him in so many words that he was dying. We had always tried to prepare him and explain the things that would happen to him. It bothered me that we had not been open with him about this. So I took his hands in mine and said, "Son, before, whenever you were sick, you would feel real bad, but then each day you would begin to feel a little bit better. Well, now you are going to get all the way better. You are going to be with Jesus in heaven."

He never answered, and I don't know for sure that he heard me. He dozed off and I must have also. At 3:00 A.M. he awoke with a start: "Ice! Get my ice. Dad! Where is my dad? *Daddy!*"

We scrambled for fresh ice. Dutch came running from the other room. "Why don't you give him the ice?" he snapped. Tempers flared; confusion set in. I had placed Todd's hands in the bowl of ice so he would know it was there, but he couldn't feel it anymore.

My sister called to say that Niqua had awakened screaming—could Mother come?

I fled from the room. In the other bedroom, I pounded my fists on the window frame: "God! I can't take it anymore! I can't stand the thought of his dying, but I can't take this anymore. You *promised!* Lord, you promised not to allow us to be tempted beyond what we're able to endure. Well, I can't endure anymore."

I sobbed. For a moment I thought I was going crazy. In that split second, it seemed that I had the choice to give in to despair and lose my mind, or take the hand of Jesus so he could pull me out of the storm-tossed waves. I trusted Jesus.

I heard Todd call me, but I couldn't go in that room anymore. Dutch came and put me to bed. It was his turn to sleep, and he was as tired as I was, but he knew I'd reached my limit.

While I slept, he and Grandpa sat with Todd, holding his hands.

16

"Honey, Todd is in heaven."

It was one hour after I had reminded God of his promise.

Dutch and I embraced and cried, and yet he detected a faint smile on my lips. I was so relieved that it was all over. The house was quiet —no more loud and labored breathing.

Dutch told me that while I had been sleeping, Todd's breaths had come further and further apart. His hands grew cold and turned blue.

Dutch prayed: "God bless you, Son. Thank you, Jesus."

And then the suffering was over.

Grandpa said: "He has been a good boy."

Dutch felt a coldness in the room. Todd's spirit had left his body.

They laid him down to make him look more comfortable and tried to close his dehydrated eyelids.

Before entering the room, I stopped at the door and breathed a prayer: "Dear God, help me to bear it. Be with me when I go in there."

I tried again to close Todd's eyes completely. As I looked at them I knew that that which was Todd was not in them anymore.

We had decided ahead of time that we would take Todd to the hospital ourselves and allow them to perform an autopsy. Perhaps it would help other children.

Dutch shaved (he sprouted a one-week beard) and got dressed while I called the doctor. Yes, he would notify the emergency room that we were bringing Todd in and he would meet us there. I called Mother and some friends.

We wrapped Todd in a blanket and I slipped into the backseat of the car with him. His lifeless head weighed so heavily on my arm. I I had draped the blanket over his face. Dutch, in a loving reflex motion, had pulled it back again.

After a 20-minute trip to the hospital, I was eager to have a nurse bring a gurney so I could place my lifeless bundle on it for her to take away.

There was paperwork. Todd was pronounced dead on arrival.

"Do you have his identification card with you?"

"No, but I do remember his number: 506679."

Then we sat in the conference room with the doctor. He served coffee and allowed us to talk.

We were interrupted time and again by nurses coming in for morning report. They apologized and withdrew, but we realized it was time to go home. A new day had started at the hospital.

When we got home, Grandma had fixed breakfast. A friend met us at the door with, "I'll bet he's already organized a baseball game in heaven." She embraced us with tears streaming down her face.

I went to Todd's room. There were his books and an untouched bottle of pain pills. The Monopoly game was set up, the dice ready to be thrown. "Little Toot" was still on the record player. It was all the same, but silent.

During breakfast Dona dropped by with some baked goods. "He is rejoicing with the Lord," she said.

Then we went to Forest Lawn to make the

arrangements. The people there had respect for our feelings. They served coffee and made suggestions. Then they left us alone to talk.

A battle was going on within me. "Nothing but the best is good enough. How can we think of cost at a time like this?" And yet it all seemed so pointless. Todd was gone. What possible difference could it make what we did with the body?

"It's out of respect for his life that we do it," Dutch said.

The counselor kept us in line by suggesting medium-cost items. He pointed out our natural desire to go overboard and advised against it.

Dutch stood on many different lots and checked the view we would have when visiting the grave. Finally he was satisfied.

Did we want flowers, and could we bring the clothes we wanted Todd to wear? Did we want a tent set up at the grave site, in case it rained? How about announcements in the papers? Who would the organist and soloist be, and how many police escorts did we need?

"You don't have to decide right now. Just let us know."

On the way home, it was my turn to cry. I was sitting by the kitchen table weeping when our neighbor came with food. My tears left her helpless to say more than "I'm sorry."

I was still weeping when Pastor Roufs arrived. My head hurt and I was exhausted. I told him that everything seemed pointless. He said we didn't need to make any more funeral arrangements that day.

"Pastor, we'd like you to think about giving an altar call at the funeral," Dutch said.

Mother lovingly transplanted Todd's favorite flowers from his garden into bowls. She added a little white angel and pictures of the statue of Christ that Todd had so often admired. None of the many fancy flower arrangements matched the beauty of Mother's creation.

After a short rest we went back to Forest Lawn.

"Todd is ready now," the hostess said. "You can go see him."

"Oh, no! Not yet! I'm not ready! . . . You go," I said to Dutch and Mother. "I'll go later. Not now. I can't."

My knees felt like butter, and my stomach was churning. How could I look at the lifeless form that had been my son? "You don't understand!" I felt like screaming. "He was once a part of me. He came from my womb. I know what he feels like, what he smells like. I can trace the contours of his hands in my mind. What will he look like now?"

They encouraged me to come along. "You'll

have to see him some time. It might as well be now."

Why couldn't the elevator be slower, the halls longer, to delay what I must face? Even at the door I pushed Mother and Dutch ahead of me and stood to the side so as to not catch a glimpse before I was ready.

"Dear God, you have to help me! I can't take this! Please go in with me. Hold my hand."

There it was—that . . . body. It had all of Todd's characteristics, but Todd wasn't there.

I grew excited. "It doesn't look like him. Praise God! I know Todd isn't here anymore! He's with the Lord. This isn't Todd. It is just what is left of him here. I'm so glad."

Later I got out pictures of Todd smiling, full of life. "That's Todd, here," I would say. "That body is not Todd."

A woman introduced herself as the one who had prepared Todd's body. She apologized that, since Todd was bald, they had not been able to camouflage the incisions on his head left by the autopsy.

Todd had been wearing his baseball cap everywhere but to bed, so we decided to put his hat on him now. No one else saw the body until the cap was in place.

We fell into bed early that night. We held each other and cried awhile, drawing on each other for strength.

160

17

Friends and neighbors brought flowers and food. Strength and joy grew within me as the day progressed.

We all felt uneasiness, fear, and dread when we went into Todd's room that day. But then Dutch knew what was wrong. "Everything that was good in this room—the guardian angels, the Holy Spirit—they left with Todd, and all that's left in the room is death itself."

He took command over the spirit of death and told it to leave in the name of Jesus! Dutch exorcised the room.

We felt such relief after that—no more fear or dread. The room was free and clear.

We met with Pastor Roufs to plan the memorial service.

"So people won't be embarrassed and the service interrupted, could you ask the congregation to bow their heads and close their eyes while we sing the Hallelujah? Those who would surrender their hearts or commit their lives to Christ could look up," Dutch suggested.

We were so grateful to Pastor Roufs for letting us choose the songs and hymns and help plan the service. It would be special indeed! We chose passages from John and Revelation that the Lord had used to prepare me for Todd's death, along with the Apostles' Creed and the 23rd Psalm.

Niqua had been staying with friends. It was time that she come home. She was happy to see us, but she knew things weren't the same.

I noticed that she wouldn't go near Todd's room. She was obviously afraid of it. I took her in my arms and together we entered the room.

"Oh, Toddy doesn't live here anymore!" She cried, wiggling free from my arms. Her relief was obvious. She skipped around the room, picking up various things.

"Mommy, how come Toddy didn't take his teddy bear to heaven with him? Why did he leave his watch? Oh, and look! His clothes are still here, too."

The simple faith of a child! Indeed! Toddy didn't live *here* anymore.

Thursday night it rained and stormed, but

Friday morning dawned bright and clear. The sky was blue and crisp, without a whisp of a cloud or a hint of smog. We could see forever.

"Sing praises to the Lord, O you his saints, and give thanks to his holy name. For his anger is but for a moment, and his favor is for a lifetime. Weeping may tarry for the night, but joy comes with the morning" (Ps. 30:4-5).

I didn't want Niqua to see Todd. As far as she knew, he was in heaven. She was too young to understand why his body had to be locked up in a box. We kept her in the pastor's office until after the casket had been closed for the last time.

Dutch and I had said our last good-byes the night before. I had planned to bend over Todd one last time and kiss him and say: "See you in the morning. Say hi to Jesus for me." But I didn't. Todd wasn't there, and I certainly didn't feel like kissing that cold body.

John wept during the service, and we could hear many sniffles behind us. Our main concern was how the altar call would go. I was so excited I could hardly wait for Pastor Roufs to get to that part of the service.

First, he paid tribute to Todd through a joyful, hope-filled sermon. It meant so much to us that I would like to share part of it.

> One of the hard, blunt facts of human existence is death. And when a child dies,

we especially feel the shattering and crushing power of death. But then we remember that God never promised that there would be no empty chairs at the table or that there would be no idle toys. Jesus has never said that he would keep every child alive until adulthood.

As we think about Todd, we remember him as a fighter. There was no giving in or giving up. And because of that element of fighting in his life, I'd like to share a passage of Scripture from 2 Corinthians 4: "We are often troubled, but not crushed; sometimes in doubt, but never in despair; there are many enemies, but we are never without a friend" (TEV). And the Phillips has this translation: "We may be knocked down but we are never knocked out."

Todd has been knocked down, but he's not knocked out. One of the things I recall about Todd is the way he would fight to do what he wanted to do. Not even cancer was going to keep him from learning or from playing. After the operation on his back, when I visited his home, he had to go out and show me how he could swing the bat and throw the ball. He kept trying.

Last Sunday I was at his home. There he was playing Monopoly, trying to beat his mother, and he didn't have enough strength to shake the dice or to move the pegs, but yet, there he was, counting the

money sharply. And then he was completely fatigued. He tipped over and lay down,
and his parents brought pillows to support
him. By the time they got the pillows there,
he wanted to be back at Monopoly. That's
the way he continued to fight and struggle
to live.

Todd has been knocked down, but he
has never been knocked out, for Todd believed in the resurrection. He believed in
the grace of God. God's grace had reached
out to him. And grace is God's love and
God's forgiveness. And it was this kind of
confidence and trust that Todd had in
Jesus Christ. If you had gone into Todd's
room the last few days, you would have
seen pictures of Jesus surrounding Todd.
And it was because of his love for Christ
that those pictures were there. Todd knew
that Jesus was his Savior.

In Mark, the tenth chapter, it says that
parents brought children to Jesus, "that he
should touch them: and his disciples re-
buked those that brought them. But when
Jesus saw it, he was much displeased, and
said unto them: Suffer the little children to
come unto me, and forbid them not: for of
such is the kingdom of God" (KJV).

Todd said this was a sad story that
turned out all right. Isn't that interpreta-
tion marvelous? People brought their children to Jesus and the disciples said, "No,

Jesus doesn't have time for children." But Jesus did. Todd knew that he was accepted and loved and belonged to Christ, because his faith was in Jesus. And one of the last days, when people wondered whether he had any strength in his hands, he took one of these Etch-a-sketches, and there in the middle of it he drew a cross. He believed, you see, that Jesus died for him and that because of that he was a child of God.

With his grandmother Todd would go to Forest Lawn quite frequently. He called it "the Jesus place," I imagine because there were so many statues of Jesus there. He wanted to see what they did with, as he said, the "leftover" bodies. One day as he and his grandmother were there, they saw people standing around a casket and over an empty grave. He wanted to go and see how the people were acting, but his grandmother said, "No, we can't do that." Then he said these words: "Someday, when I'm buried, I'll be able to look down and see how the people are acting as they stand around *my* casket." He could say that, you see, because he had this great and profound confidence and trust that "to be absent from the body is to be present with the Lord."

God's grace reached out to Todd's parents, too, Dutch and Gaby. And the ways they have shown the reality of Christ in their lives have been for us an inspiration. We have seen the vitality of their faith, and we have given thanks and praise to God.

As a congregation we have been involved in meaningful experiences with them in the past year. Remember that Sunday when we anointed Todd? Then the exhilaration that we all had upon Todd's improvement, and the Sunday evening fellowships of prayer and singing together? All of these because of God's grace operative in you. May his grace and his strength support you today and tomorrow and in the months and years ahead.

There is a marvelous statement in 2 Samuel. David, after he lost his son, says, "You cannot come to me, my son, but I can go to you." A treasured part of your lives has gone to heaven, and that, we trust, will cause you too to be more aware of things of the Spirit. We go down to difficulty and death; we go down, but we go on. We do not live as though this were the end, for Todd or for ourselves. God picks us up to carry us in his arms and send us on our way for new experiences, new conquests, new life and at last, the resurrection.

No one gets out of life alive. We all will be knocked down by death as Todd has been, but none of us has to be knocked out. Something has happened that changed

167

everything. Death has been given a death blow by Jesus Christ. The Father who has raised the Lord Jesus will raise our loved ones and will make us all to stand together in his presence. And that's possible when we accept the grace of God into our lives, when we invite the Lord Jesus into our hearts.

And so, today, the family wants you to have an opportunity to make that kind of experience yours. You can open your life to the Savior and live in his grace. So, during the singing of the Hallelujah, the family has asked that all of us bow our heads with our eyes closed, and it would be very meaningful for them if someone here today, during this service, would accept Jesus as Savior, or if some of you would recommit your lives to the Lord. If you want to make that kind of response to Christ, would you lift your eyes and look at the cross? That's the way in which you, today, can make evident that you accept Christ as your Savior.

Then "The Lord's Prayer" was sung, and I felt the Lord assuring me of his presence.

During the interment the Lord shielded me from all the pain. It seemed I was lifted high above the circumstances, wrapped in a cloud to cushion the blows.

"Thank you, Lord, for helping me the way

168

you do. I know I can't stay up here in this cloud forever. You will have to bring me down again. Please let me down gently—little by little. Don't let me crash."

God showed his love through his people in many ways. People drove as much as five hours to be near. We were also comforted by many notes and cards.

Todd truly is asleep in Jesus. I praise God for the assurance you have of this.

Your faith shines and radiates. I know the loss you feel, but the courage you have shown has meant so much to me and my family.

Thank you for letting me be part of Todd's last days.

We all loved him, but he's with Jesus Christ now and happier than we could imagine. Todd brought me closer to Christ than I've ever been.

May you and your family be truly comforted during this temporary separation from Todd. Your strength and faith during this period of testing has been a beautiful witness to all of us. I will not forget Todd's expression of faith during the short time I had the privilege of knowing him.

In the mystery of God's wisdom and power are many questions . . . and answers. Two answers out of his Word give clarity and hope in times like yours. The first, illness and disease do not come from the hand of God—yet can be used even in the endurance of their horror by God to bless others; your faith and endurance have blessed us. The second is the promise of Jesus—Todd and you will meet at another time and another place. He has gone there first to learn and develop . . . to become what God designed him to be. Someday you all shall be together. God has promised.

It is not possible for us to express our profound sorrow over Todd's passing. The last few months have placed emotional burdens on you that few of us will ever experience. We feel Todd was fortunate in that he had two remarkable parents with the strength and courage to meet his illness head on—not to back off and wallow in their own self-pity and misery.

I am so very sorry, but know you are being lightened of your burden by your faith and your many precious memories. We only hope we can be as strong as you—you two are an inspiration to me.

My heart has been bleeding for you these past weeks. However, isn't it wonderful

170

how Todd loved Jesus? He is safe and loved with him. Praise God for such faith.

The last few weeks of Todd's illness, Dutch and I had been excused from teaching Sunday school, but this Sunday I wanted to teach. The children had many questions about Todd. Many of them had been to school with him. Some of them had been to the funeral. We laid aside the regular lesson and the boys and girls gathered around me.

"Todd is dead now, isn't he?"

"How did he go to heaven?"

"Did it hurt?"

This was a perfect opportunity for me to ask, "What do you have to do to get to heaven?"

"You have to pray?"

"You have to be good?"

One little boy was definite. "Yeah! You have to be good for a *whole year!*"

That was too much to fathom. "For a whole year!" a little girl sighed.

I told them that Jesus stood knocking on the door of their hearts, and if they simply responded and invited him in to be Lord of their lives, he would grant them the right to go to heaven as a free gift. While Jesus wanted them to be good, even for a whole year, that was not the way to make it to heaven.

Todd had known that. In one Bible he had

underlined John 3:16: "For God so loved the world that he gave his only Son, that whoever believes in him should not perish but have eternal life."

18

Why must I look at Todd's pictures to remember every detail of his features? And what did he smell like? I forgot! What was it he used to say that was so cute? His voice . . . I could no longer readily remember its tone!

But how could I not remember! How could I betray my son like that? It seemed that forgetting was a second death. I couldn't allow it! I had to hang on!

Slowly and gently, God was lowering me down from my protective cloud. He took me by the hand and helped me experience the valley I had to pass through.

Just about the time I patted myself on the back and let go of Jesus' hand ("Thank you, Lord, I think I can take it from here"), I fell

173

flat on my face and wound up sobbing out my grief.

At times the thought of living many years here on earth without Todd seemed unbearable. How I longed to be in heaven with him. Even Niqua felt that way. "Why can't I be in heaven with Toddy? Why didn't he take me with him?" I identified with Paul when he said, "For me to live is Christ; to die is gain."

Dutch had done well in choosing the plot at Forest Lawn. I found much comfort in sitting there and pouring my heart out to the Lord. "God's little garden: You plant your loved ones and watch the seed of life come forth from the witness of their life and passing."

It was good to be able to talk to Dutch about my pain, and he shared his with me. Niqua, too, was able to express her feelings. "Mommy, I misses Toddy. I wish he was here."

Slowly, even as we shared our grief, healing came. Somehow we sensed that grief harbored in our hearts, unreleased, would crush us. As we reached out to share other people's burdens, God lifted ours. With the assurance that God never says no unless he has a better plan, we grew expectant to learn what that better plan was and to be part of it.

Then one day the umbilical cord was cut. I set Todd free. In place of guilt over forgotten memories, I felt profound gratitude for having been allowed to share Todd's life and having been a vessel used to show the glory and mighty power of God. I released Todd from being my son to being a child of God.

> Thou hast turned for me my mourning into dancing; thou hast loosed my sackcloth and girded me with gladness, that my soul may praise thee and not be silent. O Lord my God, I will give thanks to thee for ever (Ps. 30:11-12).

Goodnight, Son. Say hi to Jesus for me. And I'll see you in the morning.

To contact the Monsons, write P.O. Box 3112, San Clemente, Calif. 92672.